$y = 8 - 2x^2$

$8 - 2x^2 = 0$

$-2x^2 = -8$

$2x^2 = 8$

$x^2 = 4$

$\boxed{x = \pm 2}$

$\int_{-2}^{2} (8 - 2x^2) dx$

$= 8x - \frac{2x^3}{3} + \cancel{x}$

$F(2) = 8(2) - \frac{2(2)^3}{3}$

$= 16 - \frac{16}{3} \cancel{= 16 - 4 = 12} \quad \frac{48}{3} - \frac{16}{3} = \frac{32}{3}$

$F(-2) = 8(-2) - \frac{2(-2)^3}{3}$

$= -16 + \frac{16}{3} = \cancel{20} \quad \frac{-48}{3} + \frac{16}{3} = \frac{-32}{3}$

$A = F(2) - F(-2) = \cancel{[12 - (-20)] = 32}$

$\left[\frac{32}{3} - \left(-\frac{32}{3} \right) \right] = \frac{64}{3}$

Systems of Individualized Education

THE NATIONAL SOCIETY
FOR THE STUDY OF EDUCATION

Series on Contemporary Educational Issues
Kenneth J. Rehage, Series Editor

The 1975 Titles

Systems of Individualized Education, Harriet Talmage, Editor
Schooling and the Rights of Children, Vernon F. Haubrich and
  Michael W. Apple, Editors
*Educational Policy and International Assessment: Implications of
  the IEA Surveys of Achievement*, Alan C. Purves and Daniel U.
  Levine, Editors

The National Society for the Study of Education also publishes Year-books which are distributed by the University of Chicago Press. Inquiries regarding all publications of the Society, as well as inquiries about membership in the Society, may be addressed to the Secretary-Treasurer, 5835 Kimbark Avenue, Chicago, IL 60637. Membership in the Society is open to any who are interested in promoting the investigation and discussion of educational questions.

Systems
of
Individualized
Education

Edited by
Harriet Talmage
University of Illinois
Chicago Circle

McCutchan Publishing Corporation
2526 Grove Street
Berkeley, California 94704

ISBN O-8211-1904-4

Library of Congress Catalog Card Number 74-24478

Series Foreword

One of the continuing searches in education has been for ways of accommodating instruction to the well-known facts about the nature and extent of individual differences. Advances in technology have now made possible an approach to this problem that could not have been envisioned two decades ago. In this volume three "systems" of individualized instruction, each of which leans in some degree upon the new technologies, are described by those primarily responsible for their development.

The volume does more than presenting these descriptions. It provides a review of psychological theories bearing on the issue of individualization, an analysis of the implications of individualized instruction from the standpoint of those interested in curriculum design, and some critical commentaries. Like other books in the Series on Contemporary Educational Issues, this volume has been prepared in the hope that it will stimulate informed discussion of an important current development in education.

Other titles in the 1975 Series on Contemporary Educational Issues, published under the auspices of the National Society for the Study of Education, are:

v

Educational Policy and International Assessment: Implications of the IEA Surveys of Achievement, edited by Alan C. Purves and Daniel U. Levine;
Schooling and the Rights of Children, edited by Vernon F. Haubrich and Michael W. Apple.

The Society is indebted to Professor Talmage, editor of this volume, and to the contributors who graciously responded to her request for original chapters for the book.

Kenneth J. Rehage

for the Committee on the Expanded
Publication Program of the
National Society for the Study
of Education

Preface

In selecting an area in curriculum and instruction for the "Series on Contemporary Educational Issues," the committee members were wary of presenting a "current innovation" that explodes on to the educational scene, holds center stage for a brief period, and quietly fades away. As a pragmatic nation we like our problems solved with dispatch and tend to look for cure-all solutions to complex educational issues. In many, if not most, cases the innovations collapse after the initial period of enthusiasm for a number of reasons: lack of conceptual focus; failure to understand the effects of change on a system; lack of attention to organizational details for implementation; unrealistic appraisal of costs and their effects on other educational priorities; and a heavy reliance on the interest, time, and energy of extraordinary teachers and administrators.

Educational responses to individual differences are a recurring theme in American education. Over time a body of serious literature, empirical and philosophical, from a number of disciplines has contributed substantively to an understanding of individual differences and their implications for curriculum and instruction. A review of past yearbooks of the National Society for the Study of Education documents the continued interest. Efforts at research, development, and implementation over the past eight years have been addressed to many of the problems raised in the yearbooks.

In surveying present responses to individualization at the elementary and secondary levels, we find three major research and development efforts that appear to rise above faddism: Individually Guided Education (IGE), Adaptive Environments for Learning (an extension of the initial system referred to as Individually Prescribed Instruction [IPI]), and Planning for Learning in Accordance with Needs (PLAN*). Each of these systems has a conceptual focus, acknowledges the interpersonal ramifications of change on a school, gives attention to the organizational support for implementation, and is not overly dependent on extraordinary staff to make the system functional. Cost is still a problem but one that is not insurmountable and need not jeopardize the design of the systems.

The intent of this volume is to bring to the reader's attention serious efforts to respond to the demand for individualization. The senior authors of the three chapters on individualized systems worked on their respective systems at the conceptual phase and guided them through the research and development phases. The editor instructed the authors to present a description of their programs and to call attention to the ways in which these systems, operating within the context of functioning school environment, are responsive to demands for individualization. The authors of the other five chapters were selected because of their interest and effort in understanding the curricular, instructional, and evaluation implications of individualization on schooling. Professor Eash assumed the task of guiding the readers through the volume by putting the parts into a larger frame of reference. He reminds us all of the continuing dilemma confronting every educator: how are societal and individual purposes to be balanced in educational programs?

Harriet Talmage

Contributors

Leslie J. Briggs, Professor of Instructional Design and Development, Florida State University

Harvey J. Brudner, President, PLAN*, Westinghouse Learning Corporation

Maurice J. Eash, Professor of Education and Director of the Office of Evaluation Research, University of Illinois, Chicago Circle

John C. Flanagan, President and Director, American Institutes for Research

Robert Glaser, Professor of Psychology and Education and Co-Director, Learning Research and Development Center, University of Pittsburgh

Herbert J. Klausmeier, V. A. C. Henmon Professor of Educational Psychology and Director, Wisconsin Research and Development Center for Cognitive Learning, University of Wisconsin, Madison

Robert W. Marker, Vice-President, Marketing, Westinghouse Learning Corporation

Jerome Rosner, Associate Professor of Education and Research Associate, and Project Director, Perceptual Skills, Learning Research and Development Center, University of Pittsburgh

Louis J. Rubin, Professor of Education, University of Illinois, Urbana

Michael Scriven, Professor of Philosophy, University of California, Berkeley

William M. Shanner, Principal Research Scientist, American Institutes for Research

Harriet Talmage, Professor of Education, University of Illinois, Chicago Circle

Herbert J. Walberg, Professor of Human Development and Learning, University of Illinois, Chicago Circle

Contents

Introduction

Maurice J. Eash

Approaches to the individualization of instruction have a lengthy history. Evidence to support these approaches has been available in the annals of psychology for at least fifty years. But the relationship of evidence on the nature and extent of individual differences to the development of instructional programs that take those differences into account has not been a simple linear one. The educational literature is strewn with plans that were developed on a small scale but were not able to be generalized to mass education. Only in the last decade has research and development produced sufficient technology to bring individualized instruction into the realm of possibility for large numbers of students and for total school systems.

But one cannot assume that the development of technology leads immediately to individualized instruction. Before complex systems could be built, limited theory and simplistic instructional paradigms required extension and verification. For this reason the reader will find it helpful to view this book as composed of three sections.

First, a historical and functional framework of psychology and instructional design is presented in Chapters 1 and 2 to provide the reader with an in-depth background in preparation for an intensive look at three systems of individualized instruction.

Second, Chapters 3, 4, and 5 provide descriptions of those systems, which were constructed by team efforts and with heavy developmental funding from the federal government. The systems are currently being used by thousands of students in hundreds of school systems. While they start from similar premises concerning instructional design, each system emphasizes different facets. Adaptive Environments for Learning emphasizes diagnosis and materials; IGE (Individually Guided Education) stresses school reorganization, a recasting of classroom structure and instructional roles; and PLAN* (Program for Learning in Accordance with Needs) is focused on a system of organizing materials and a system of management using extant instructional materials. Because each of the systems formulates an instructional approach into a comprehensive curriculum design, detail becomes a problem to the reader's understanding of the conceptual framework. Thus, a clear understanding of Chapters 1 and 2 will aid in comprehending the systems described in Chapters 3, 4, and 5, and in guiding the reader in the commentaries on issues regarding individualization in succeeding chapters.

Third, in Chapters 6, 7, and 8 the authors view individualized instruction from different perspectives. Building a system for individualization has been an enormous undertaking, one that has imposed evolving solutions on age-old instructional problems. Producing a viable system has not meant the satisfactory solution of the persistent problems.[1] The pushing back of the frontier of theory and practice has, rather, further revealed a vast continent of unknowns. In Chapter 6 Briggs identifies common elements in the three programs and makes a number of suggestions for developers of future systems. After a selective tour of the literature on affect and emotion, Rubin provides in Chapter 7 a "feel" for a series of dilemmas faced by those interested in affective education. In view of the heavy emphasis on cognitive objectives within these three systems, the desire for more direct approaches to instruction that have greater affective tone will strike sympathetic chords in many readers, but it will also heighten ambivalence about increasing the ambiguity of the instructional systems through introduction of less specific objectives open to more diverse interpretation. By definition, a system sets restraints and defines boundaries which Rubin explores in the search for a design for affective education.

In Chapter 8 Scriven places the individualization of instruction in a context of some major political and economic questions facing public education. He rightly focuses on the mundane but continuing issue of financial support. If individualized instruction means sharply increased costs it will, he predicts, rapidly fall from the favor of a tax-burdened public. In addition, the superiority of total systems of individualization over piecemeal approaches to individualization has not been empirically demonstrated. The reader may find particularly provocative Scriven's search for standards of evaluation and for comparative data.

Viewed as a whole, the book lays out a well-marked road for individualizing instruction in schools. Moreover, it gives a description of the present status of advanced systems and also looks ahead to probable future developments and into instructional terrain that will test the assumptions of current developers. Systems of individualization are, in a sense, the instructional developers' counterpart of the journey to the moon—no mean achievement for earthbound mortals who long related only poetically to that circling satellite. Developments in theory and technology leaped over historically insurmountable barriers, giving us a new perspective on the relationship between moon and earth. But once the glow of achievement had dimmed the question "to what end?" pressed in again. In this book we see a technology for the "engineering" of instruction. The ends we pursue are not nearly as clear.

As we move toward mastery of the technology for individualization, we need to consider a number of larger questions about educational goals for an individual and a society. Only one broad query along these lines is posed here: do individualized approaches to instruction promote individual achievement in isolation from social responsibility?

The interdependence of individuals is an increasing fact of life internationally as well as nationally. Does the individual, who is nourished on a curriculum devoted to building his individual competencies devoid of reference to a social context, build a sense of awareness and responsibility for his fellowmen? Other systems of education place their emphasis upon group efforts and societal goals with a downgrading of individual achievement. Is a "cult of the individual" a potential product of an exclusive emphasis on individualization? And, more importantly, can the society maintain itself where individual private interests are always preeminent over public-societal interests? With the increase in world population and the pressure on natural resources becoming more acute, "doing your own thing" without forethought to social consequences is a luxury that we can ill afford. It is unlikely that we shall be able to extend linearly the present consumer orientation to burn as much petroleum as we can buy, cover as much fertile agricultural soil with concrete and houses as we can economically command, and let the fashion of the marketplace rather than function dictate the allocation of resources. To retain for the individual the freedom of choice on matters that have been treated as private decisions, but that have major social consequences when viewed in the larger scene, is one of the crucial issues facing us today.

To build a system of education is to help cast the future citizen. In the current efforts to build instructional systems one is struck by the silence on societal goals and the contribution of the school curriculum to their achievement. To understand the systems in individualized instruction is the responsibility of every educator, for as means they also shape the ends of education. And as we gather the means we need to think deeply about the quality of life and the meanings we seek as ends.

Note

1. For a description and analysis of these pervasive problems, see "Evaluating Instructional Systems: PLAN*, IGE and IPI," *EPIE Educational Products Report* 58 (New York: Educational Products Information Exchange Institute, 1974).

1. Psychological Theories of Educational Individualization

Herbert J. Walberg

This chapter treats three main topics, with sections of various lengths devoted to each. The first section, deservedly very brief, derives instructional implications from dictionary definitions of the term "individualization." It shows the confusion and conflicting implications that reside in ordinary meanings of the term and the need for analytic models to deal fully with the complexity of the educational issues. The second section, somewhat longer but in relation to the importance of the topic admittedly brief, illustrates the historical development of psychological theories from the continental and Anglo-American traditions and synthetic movements. It points out how instructional practices follow from psychological theories about the child's nature and growth. The third section, the longest, presents a taxonomy of psychological models of instruction that may be found in educational practice and evaluated through applied research. An attempt is made to ensure the taxonomy is reasonably systematic in the senses of considering all cases and mutual exclusion and to make the models scientifically identifiable (although "ideal types" may not be often found) in terms of operational definitions.

Dictionary Definitions

The word "individualization" is, of course, related to "individual-ism"—"a social theory advocating the liberty, rights, or independent action of the individual," which contrasts with collectivism and in-stitutionalism, according to *Webster's*. Since the common meanings of such abstract words evolve through generations, they can cause great misunderstanding unless they are made explicit and opera-tional. For example, "liberal" had once implied the precedence of individual liberty over other ideals such as social equality and justice; more recently the word appears to imply federal programs for solving social problems.

Table 1-1 shows Webster's definitions of "individualization." The instructional implications derived from the definitions suggest a num-ber of questions: Does the child possess native individuality, or must he be made individual? Are the same or different means of education appropriate for different children? Are the same or different educa-tional ends suitable for different children? Who determines the ends and means? The answers may seem obvious to some, and the ques-tions themselves may seem to be semantic niceties to others. But some of the large controversial questions in education today hinge upon the answers given. For example, the idea that education should provide equality of opportunity had grown in America since Jefferson, and educators of a few decades ago would have considered recent research and policy questions extremely naive or leftist. In the 1960s some asked if education should produce equality of test re-sults. In the 1970s some asked if it should produce equality of in-comes.[1] These issues go beyond psychology. Our aim here is to gain some understanding of the historical development of the psycholog-ical traditions of individualization and to derive models from the traditions that are represented in educational practice. Table 1-1 makes it clear that our understanding must include the ends, means, and control of the educational process.

Psychological Traditions

More often than philosophers and sociologists, psychologists and educators are apt to forget their theoretical forebears and practical precursors. With a few crude strokes, one can sketch the evolution of

Table 1-1
Dictionary definitions of individualization and related educational implications

Definition	Implication
1. a. To make individual in character; invest with individuality.	Implies instructional activity aimed at a predetermined end unique to each individual but not necessarily determined by him. Might deny both equality of result and equality of opportunity. Might deny initial individuality of student in implying that he must be made individual.
b. To treat or notice individually; particularize, specify.	"To treat" is not specific with regard to ends or means nor with regard to opportunity for or result of instruction. The remainder of the definition and definition lc both imply passive perceptions and are even less specific.
c. To distinguish.	
2. To put into the hands or management of an individual.	Suggests allowing the student to develop by himself the means and ends of his education. Might deny teacher and parent preferences and allow collectivist or standardized means and ends in conflict with definition la.
3. To adjust or adapt (as a treatment of justice) to the needs or special circumstances of an individual.	Implies alternative means but leaves open the possibility of fixed ends, possibly collectivist or standardized. Might deny student a role in the determination of ends and means.

Source: Webster's Third New International Dictionary (1970), where the definitions are listed in order of common, central meanings.

individualization and show that what appears wholly new today is usually either a new combination of ideas or a revival of older patterns, notwithstanding some technological innovations. The purpose of such an exercise is neither to blame nor praise contemporary instructional theorists and developers but to illustrate how psychology and instruction reflect old traditions as well as the current zeitgeist. Needless to say, the sketch must oversimplify and skip over much detailed material.

The Continental Tradition

Tables 1-2, 1-3, and 1-4 are analyses of Riegel's[2] review of some influences of ideology on developmental psychology with supplementary points (indicated with asterisks) added for our purposes from Boring[3] and elsewhere.[4] Table 1-2 represents the continental European tradition which derives from Socrates and Plato, whose mind-matter dualism and theory of education as internal apprehension of eternal ideas by stages ("All knowledge is but remembrance") portrayed the teacher as the midwife of ideas inherent in the child's mind. The tradition emphasizes the uniqueness of the child and qualitative, structural models of mental growth. It has led to educational applications that are child centered or child directed in varying degrees and different forms; Rousseau's romantic ideal of the child's inherent nobility is one extreme of the tradition. From the continental perspective, the child's progress is based on standards relevant to his needs, age, culture, and experience, and the structuring and integration of knowledge (rather than breaking it into discrete elements) are stressed.

The Anglo-American Tradition

Table 1-3 presents some leading figures and ideas in the Anglo-American tradition which derives from Aristotle's notion of learning as the association of mental elements (only one part of his theory of mind). Although the continental tradition in the forms of gestalt psychology (emphasizing cognitive structures) and dynamic psychology (emphasizing affective structures) has made occasional inroads, elementism and its close colleague, behaviorism, are the overriding forces in psychology as it is generally taught in American universities. (Elementism, however, is generally less dominant in social, clinical, and developmental psychology than it is in psychometrics and

Table 1-2
Continental European tradition of learning theory

Source	Theory
*Descartes (1596-1650)	Sharp Platonic dualism of ideas and observables; subjective introspection of innate ideas; because knowledge develops from within the child, the teacher is superfluous.
Leibniz (1646-1716) Hegel (1770-1831)	Stages of developmental progression of individual and cultural development; generational and cultural differences emphasized.
Rousseau (1712-1778)	Child as "noble savage" to be educated and evaluated in view of peer group standards; since adult society corrupts the child's inherent goodness, his natural state should be preserved; also, men as equals in primitive society.
*Kant (1724-1804)	Logical a priori categories of human understanding that order objects of external reality.
Pestalozzi (1746-1827)	Education appropriate to the individual child; specially trained teachers required.
Froebel (1782-1852)	Child as unfolding flower; teacher as gardener providing conditions for unhindered growth; child-centered approach to kindergarten; in practice, however, some of his instructional methods might be termed "prescriptive."
Montessori (1870-1952)	Rationalistic, goal-directed but child-initiated, child-paced education; self-correcting instructional materials reveal structure of external reality.
*Freud (1856-1939)	Acquisition of mental structures by steps (id, ego, superego) through resolution of psychosexual conflicts in childhood; mental mechanisms such as repression and sublimation; diversity and deviance such as slips and blocks present and even necessary in "normal" development.
Spranger (1882-1963)	Diversity of individual and cultural values; education based on phenomenology, empathy, and sensitivity; child not to be evaluated on basis of adult society; youth led by youth.
Piaget (1968)	Child characterized not by continuous development but by development by steps or stages, each of which must be evaluated by its own standards; emphasis on progression through maturation and interaction with natural environment rather than contrived stimulation such as instruction.

Note: For living theorists, reference dates are given rather than years of birth and death. Names with asterisks have been added to Riegel's lists.

experimental and educational psychology in Europe and the United States.) The characteristic research methodology on the Continent is an intensive, longitudinal case study of one or a few children, though there are notable exceptions such as the French psychologist Binet, the founder of mental measurement. Anglo-American psychology employs statistical analysis of cross-sectional data on large numbers of subjects or of closely manipulated or controlled experiments.[5]

Table 1-3
Anglo-American tradition of learning theory

Source	Theory
Hobbes (1588-1679)	Individuals, egotistically motivated and engaged in a struggle against one another, require a "social contract" to establish security, property rights, and a measure of freedom.
*Locke (1632-1704)	Mind as "blank tablet"; development and education as acquisition and association of elements or items of knowledge.
Darwin (1809-1882)	Species improve over many generations through competition and selection; the survivors are ideally suited to the environment.
Spencer (1820-1903) Sumner (1840-1910) Pearson (1857-1936)	Ideal cultures and ideal individuals compete, survive, and dominate; nonstandard groups and deviant individuals are defective; children as incomplete adults.
Galton (1822-1911)	Heredity determines measurable human and group quality.
Hall (1846-1924)	Individual shaped mainly by genetic factors until adolescence and by environment thereafter; hence both are important.
*Thorndike (1874-1949)	Curriculum divided into elements; educational growth measured by items on objective tests.
Gesell (1880-1961) Terman (1887-1956)	Hall's students who continued research in Galton vein and developed quantitative behavioral norms and psychometric standards.

Note: Names with asterisks have been added to Riegel's lists.

The data for statistical analysis are discrete elements of behavior (often summed) such as categorized responses to external stimuli or coded answers to items on questionnaires and multiple-choice, "objective" tests. The dominance of this research methodology in American universities should not be underestimated; for example, on this side of the Atlantic elementist research methods are typically applied to the ideas of continental-structural theorists such as Spranger, Freud, and Piaget.

The Anglo-American model of mental growth emphasizes continuous amassing of elements of response potential, often on a single standard such as intelligence or achievement. Proponents of heredity and environment, both within the Anglo-American tradition, have struggled with one another intermittently for the last half century, but many in both camps do not question the idea of a unitary measure of mental growth.[6] Living in a more stratified society, the English (and Americans who have studied in England such as Arthur Jensen) have favored hereditarian explanations of mental development. Americans have normally combined elementism with optimism and pragmatism and advocated environmental explanations and interventions. The issues in the struggle appear alien to many psychologists on the Continent; they have less often entered the argument and have adhered more closely to individual cases. Many appear to believe that the child will progress naturally in the conventional environments of the home and school without extraordinary interventions or that the child himself can help shape his environment.

Synthetic Movements

Table 1-4 contains syntheses of parts of the continental and Anglo-American traditions of developmental psychology. None of the ideas is a grand theory or overarching synthesis of the disparate parts within or across the traditions; much more theoretical and empirical work is necessary before we can formulate that type of theory. But it can be said that such syntheses put forward in the past have sometimes led to important educational ideologies and reforms. John Dewey comes to mind. Early in his career he reacted against Kant's a priori categories of mind and the structural notion of the progression of history by stages, took issue with the German-trained Titchener's structural psychology, and argued for pragmatism, instrumentalism, and experimentation.[7] Such ideas in his voluminous

Table 1-4
Movements toward synthesis of continental and Anglo-American traditions of learning theory

Source	Theory
*Herbart (1776-1841)	Mind as dynamic interplay of external and internalized ideas; instruction as assimilation of new ideas into totality of conscious ideas or "apperceptive mass."
*James (1842-1910)	Consciousness as personal and changing; each conscious state a function of the entire psycho-physical reality; mind as cumulative rather than recurrent.
Uexküll (1864-1944)	Ecology as study of interaction of organism with natural environment.
Lewin (1890-1944)	Psychology as study of person in relation to "life-space" and surrounding perceptual environment.
Piaget (1968)	Child development as product of the dialectic of accommodation of child to object and assimilation of object to child leading to successive adaptions. Since learning proceeds in irreversible stages, two types of instruction are futile: that which centers on a stage later than one the child has not completely mastered and that which centers on a stage the child has already completely mastered.
*Murray (1938)	Importance of both the "objective" environment as observed by the psychologist and the subject's perception in understanding personality development.
Brunswik (1949)	Importance of distal and proximal stimuli and subject's subjective perception of them.
Barker and Wright (1951)	Adaptation of subject to changing stimuli in the "behavior setting"; adaptation of setting to subject.
*Cronbach (1957) *Cronbach and Snow (1974)	Psychology must integrate separate traditions of individual differences and stimulus qualities; education can exploit "aptitude-treatment interactions," tendencies for different treatments to benefit different students differentially.
*Bloom (1963)	Impact of environment greatest on individual development during the early and most rapid periods of growth; importance of home environment during the first six years of life for intellectual development.
*Walberg (1971) *Walberg and Marjoribanks (1974)	Person-environment interactions; different home environments produce different growth patterns of multiple abilities in different children; student and teacher as collaborative judges of appropriateness of environment and of instructional means and goals.

Note: For living theorists, reference dates are given rather than years of birth and death. Names with asterisks have been added to Riegel's list.

writings were of course adopted by advocates of progressive education. Continental psychology has, on the other hand, also undergirded educational reforms in United States. Bruner's emphasis on the structure of the subject matter and (loosely from Piaget) the stagewise restructuring of the child's mind inspired large-scale curriculum projects sponsored by the National Science Foundation during the 1960s.

Thus philosophers and psychologists have occasionally tried to put their ideas to direct use in the schools. Their experiences have sometimes led them to reformulate their theories. A striking case is that of Wittgenstein, one of the most seminal philosophers of this century, who spent six years between his two periods of philosophical writing as a teacher of poor children in two isolated villages in the mountains of Austria. As a young man he went to Cambridge and, while studying the paradoxes posed by Bertrand Russell, came to the radical empiricist's views of the world as composed of objects arranged as facts and of language as a mirror of elements of the external world. He admitted the possibility of a range of applicability of statements, but rejected continental theories of types and categories. After enlisting and fighting on the Continent in World War I, he cast off a large family inheritance and began his teaching in Austria. Like Paul Lazarsfeld, Egon Brunswik, Else Frenkel-Brunswik, Konrad Lorenz, Edward Tolman, and Jean Piaget he came under the influence of the Viennese structural psychologist Karl Bühler. In a fascinating investigation of the "lost years," Bartley describes how Wittgenstein, impressed by the Austrian school reform movements, tried to exploit the children's interest, to relate their school work to village life, to integrate and connect the subject matter, and to get the reticent mountain children to think critically and to participate actively in the lessons instead of learning by rote.[8] He got a few of his better students into the university, but in the end he gave up school teaching and concluded that the poor are inferior to the rich and are not as intelligent, healthy, or lovable. His philosophical thinking during this period, however, had undergone profound change as revealed in his writings begun upon his return to Cambridge in 1929. He abandoned much of his early argument of one-to-one correspondences of elements of language and objects of reality and emphasized the continental ideas of contextualism, configurationism, and structure.

The future of the continental and Anglo-American psychologies and their educational applications are unclear. Nor can it be said that they have been synthesized, for while Individually Guided Education, Adaptive Environments for Learning, and Project PLAN* (described in subsequent chapters) draw mainly on the Anglo-American tradition, "open education" (described briefly in a later section of this chapter) appears to represent the rediscovery and partial assimilation of continental ideas by English and American educators. Psychological theories will probably continue to reinforce and conflict with one another, and new patterns of instruction will no doubt continue to evolve out of the current ideological zeitgeist. Following this brief historical overview of psychological theories,[9] we shall consider some psychological models of individualization explicitly or implicitly assumed in contemporary materials of instruction.

Models Assumed in Instruction

Traditional Models

The major models[10] for individualizing learning are depicted in Figures 1-1 and 1-2. Three models in Figure 1-1 have been traditionally proposed: selection, enrichment, and acceleration. Selection has two variants: eugenic, originally proposed by Plato, and selection for instruction, most commonly used in higher education, especially in Europe, in which the "unfit" are simply not accepted. Both variants are potent enough, but for the many educators who do not wish to reject the unborn or the "unfit," they are essentially conservative and defeatist doctrines.

Enrichment and acceleration are presently the most common methods for individualizing learning. In both models, there are series of activity units and tests and generally a final examination (see Figure 1-1). Students move through the same course of instruction in the same sequence; the student must, in most cases, repeat the entire course if he is judged a failure. In enrichment programs, the most common of all, every student spends the same amount of time in learning, and individual variability is evidenced in normally distributed test scores on unit and posttest criteria that correlate with measures of aptitude and environment. In sharp contrast, acceleration (some variants are called "mastery learning") ideally means that the criterion is fixed and, as a consequence, time spent by each

Model	Course of instruction	Characteristics			
		Time spent in learning	Posttest criterion	Aptitude-criterion relation	Environment-criterion relation
Traditional					
Selection					
Eugenic					
For instruction					
Enrichment	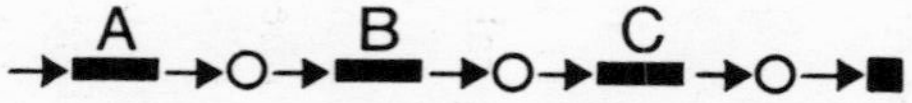	Fixed	Variable	Positive	Positive
Acceleration	Same as enrichment	Variable	Fixed	Zero	Positive
Diagnostic					
Hierarchical	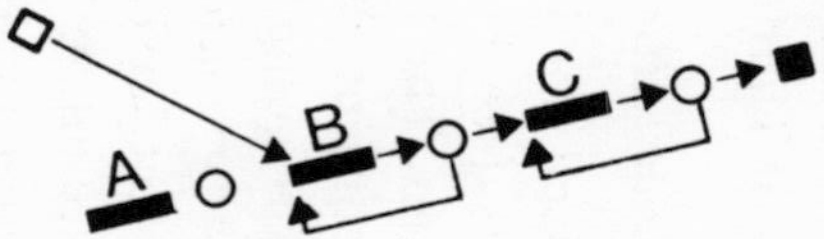	Variable	Fixed	Zero	Positive
Random	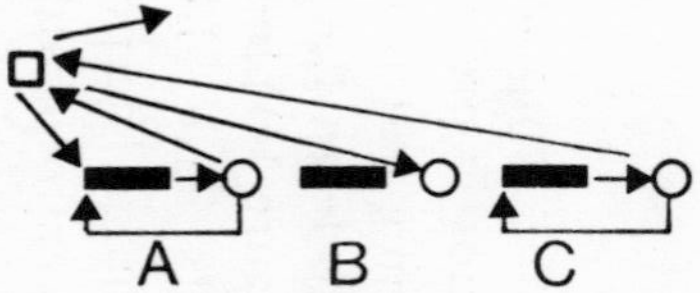	Variable	Fixed	Zero	Positive

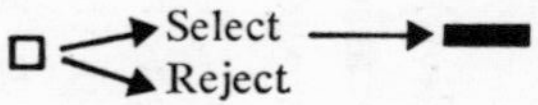

Key: Pretest □; Posttest criterion ■
— Unit of instruction
O— Unit test

Figure 1-1

Some models for individualizing instruction (from Herbert J. Walberg, "Models for Optimizing and Individualizing School Learning," *Interchange* 2 [1971] : 15-27)

Course of Instruction

Multimodal   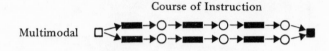

Multivalent   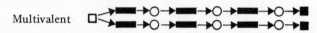

Note. The Courses of Instruction may have variants of any of those shown in Figure 1-1.

Figure 1-2

Additional models for individualizing instruction (from Walberg, "Models for Optimizing and Individualizing School Learning")

student varies. It is surprising, however, that reviews of classroom research by Strang[11] and Stephens[12] conclude that there is little relation between time spent in instruction and achievement. Both enrichment and acceleration with their emphasis on units and elements are well within the mainstream of Anglo-American psychology, more specifically that of Thorndike.

Diagnostic Models

Two recently emphasized methods for individualizing learning employ diagnostic pretests (see Figure 1-1) to assess achievements before beginning instruction. The hierarchical model assumes that it is necessary to learn the content elements of one unit of instruction (say A, in Figure 1-1) before going on to the next (B and C) and that some students have already mastered some units of instruction before beginning. The pretest serves, therefore, to place the student at the most appropriate point in the sequence of instruction. His progress is measured after each unit, and if he fails any unit, he must repeat that unit before proceeding on to the next. An example of this model is the preliminary form of Developing Mathematical Process which, in addition to unit tests, makes use of continuous monitoring of the performance of students.[13] The hierarchical model can be traced to continental notions of mental development by stages although it does emphasize splitting up the subject matter.

The random model assumes that the elements of learning need not be presented in a particular sequence; some students, for instance, may need instruction in units A and C but not in B. (See Figure 1-1.) Diagnostic pretests are given before instruction to determine which units to assign to which students. An example of this model is the Wisconsin Prototypic System of Reading Skill Development, which employs criterion-referenced tests to diagnose specific reading difficulties so as to permit appropriate assignment of units of instruction to particular students.[14] The random model is Anglo-American in emphasizing elements rather than structures.

Multimodal and Multivalent Models

The models presented in Figure 1-1 require only one basic course of instruction, although there are variants in its use. Figure 1-2 shows two models that require multiple courses of instruction.

In the first model, the multimodal, there are several courses of instruction all leading to the same achievement goal. Students are administered a pretest to determine their level of aptitude (for example, prior achievement, learning styles, and preferences), and each is assigned to the course of instruction best suited to his aptitude. Or students might be left to select their own courses. This model assumes that aptitudes interact with educational treatments; much research in the last few years has been directed toward such interactions. "Aptitude-treatment interactions" have, unfortunately, been difficult to find. Bar-Yam, in a 231-item review, found some replicated evidence that bright, flexible, and assertive students perform better when instructional methods are flexible and require independence than do their counterparts in more structured settings.[15] But aptitude-instruction interactions so far appear to account for little variance in achievement compared to the main effects of aptitude and environment, and it is likely that, if they are indeed powerful, their influence would have been uncovered by now. It is important, nevertheless, that the search continue since much theorizing about individualization seems to be based on the premise.[16] Multimodal instruction is a recent ramification of Anglo-American psychology in that it generally stresses elementist criteria of learning.

An example of a course that in theory might make use of the multimodal model is the Biological Sciences Curriculum Study.[17] Although there is no predetermined system for student assignment, there are different sequences of instruction for teaching the same general goals: the blue version represents the molecular approach; the yellow version, the systematic, taxonomic approach; and the green, the ecological approach. There are also special sequences for able and for less able students. The use of interest and ability pretests would permit appropriate assignments to sequences if aptitude-instruction interactions are found.

The other model in Figure 1-2 is termed multivalent. This model assumes (or is based on the value judgment) that not only should there be different sequences of instruction but that they should lead to different goals for different students. Harvard Project Physics was deliberately based on these premises; it was felt that different teachers and students might elect to pursue different goals in physics, say mathematical mastery or understanding the nature and history of scientific methods.[18] To permit cooperative planning, both teacher and student guides describe the course organization, various objectives, and alternative instructional activities. The multivalent model is compatible with continental psychology.

It should be noted that the acceleration, random, hierarchical, and multimodal models require a large base of data and rapid feedback for assigning students to instruction. Thus, they would depend on reliable, valid, and efficient testing or monitoring as well as on an effective system for quick summarization of data for decision making. The continuing pervasiveness of enrichment models in contemporary schools, despite alternatives advocated by theorists, may, indeed, be attributable to the lack of well-developed management systems for instruction. To be feasible, such a system of management may require an extensive data-processing system at its base.

Grouping for Instruction

Another way to examine models for optimization and individualization is to look at their organization for grouping students. Table 1-5 describes individual, small-group, and large-group organizations for instruction and their industrial analogs, and gives examples of how each organization has been used in education. It can be noted that each organization makes a different assumption about what we know about the nature of learners. Is the psychological science of man "idiographic" (to use Allport's terms), wherein the individual is sui generis, or "nomothetic," wherein generalizations may be made

Table 1-5
Grouping for instruction

Grouping	Assumption about student	Analog in industry	Per unit cost	Management sophistication	Example in education
Individual	Particular—each learns according to his own aptitude (rate, style)	Unit production—crafts, cottage industries, prototypes	High	Low	Socrates, Mark Hopkins, tutoring, independent learning
Small group	Generalization — subgroups of students sharing the same levels of aptitude can be identified	Mass production — batch production, differentiated assembly lines	Medium	Medium	Ability and interest grouping, small discussion sections, work groups
Large group	Universal—all students in group share the same levels of aptitude	Process production—intermittent chemical production in multi-purpose plant, continuous flow production of liquids, gases	Low	High	Military and industrial training, large lecture classes

Source: Walberg, "Models for Optimizing and Individualizing School Learning."

about groups of men or universal statements may be made about all men?

Table 1-5 also indicates that industry has progressively moved from expensive unit production with primitive but tailored management to mass and process production with sophisticated management, and thus to lower costs per unit with standard procedures for all units.[19] In the educational analogy, the "management" would be, say, the lecturer or computer in the large-group model, a tutor or the student himself in the individual model. The endurance of the group of class size may suggest it is a good, economic compromise and possibly that it may have psychological properties such as cooperation, cohesiveness, and competition that are attractive and conducive to some aspects of learning.[20]

The foregoing models raise a number of conceptual and practical questions concerning optimization and individualization of learning. However crude and tentative, they sharpen a number of instructional issues and identify the assumptions implicit in current programs of instruction as well as in prototypic programs and management systems now being developed. The remaining aspect of individualization to be presented is the control of the instructional processes. The subsequent discussion describes "open education," an interesting continental-style alternative to the mainstream of current American instructional practice.

Controlling Instruction

Table 1-6 pertains to the relative contributions of the teacher, the child, and instructional materials to the control of the scope, goals, pace, sequence, and means of instruction. The first cell represents the educational descendants of Rousseau; aside from the variants in the table, the romantic extreme of the university student of the late 1960s as "noble savage" or uncorrupted revolutionary capable of enlightening his professors and other radical youth movements around the world can be mentioned as extreme cases. The fourth cell represents control of instruction by the teacher. As implied by the note to the table, pure forms of any of the types are probably rare; for example, "traditional" teachers sometimes make use of children's ideas. The second cell is the case in which neither the teacher nor the student has much control; a fixed curriculum and related instructional materials dominate the teacher (if any), the student, and the

Table 1-6
Analysis of instructional control

Contribution of child	Contribution of teacher	
	Low	High
High	1. Laissez-faire, free schools, youth groups and movements; "de-schooling society"	3. Open education, integrated day, informal education, developmental classroom
Low	2. Programmed instruction; centralized curriculum planning as in some urban school systems, Japan, and European countries with authoritarian central ministries, some computer-based systems, aspects of orthodox Montessori	4. Traditional British and American education in its more authoritarian forms

Source: This fourfold classification and the first examples within each cell are from A. M. Bussis and E. A. Chittenden, *Analysis of an Approach to Open Education* (Princeton, N.J.: Educational Testing Services, 1970); the other examples are added for purposes of further illustration; none of the examples is an "ideal type."

learning process. The Far East provides many examples of long-enduring civilizations that have revered texts and other written materials. Weber, for example, attributed the continuity of Chinese culture for thousands of years to the memorization of Confucian classics, mastery of calligraphy, and rigorous examinations required of candidates for the priestly Mandarin class that administered the Empire until well into the twentieth century.[21] Perhaps the stability and resistance to change in India and the Arab world are partly attributable to habits of mind acquired by memorizing the Vedas, the Koran, and other religious writings among the intellectual classes. In Western countries where rapid change is likely to continue, there may be dangers of training (mechanical inculcation of facts and skills) by teachers, programmed materials, television, or computers. As Whitehead warned, "The result of training is that qualities essential at a later stage of a career are apt to be stamped out at an earlier stage. This is only an instance of a more general fact, that necessary technical excellence can only be acquired by training which is apt to damage those energies of mind which should direct the technical skill. This is a key fact of education, and the reason for most of its difficulties."[22] It should be noted, on the other hand, that Whitehead asserts rather than proves his point. Perhaps the wisest course is to suspend judgment on the question of relative emphasis given to higher and lower levels of cognition encouraged at different age levels. Perhaps also, until strong evidence on the question is secured, educators might well accept another of Whitehead's points: the important thing is to sustain "the rhythm of education" in alternating the two forms of cognition and showing the children the connections between the two.

Open Education

The cell remaining to be discussed pertains to open education. Since it offers interesting continental contrasts with the three instructional systems presented in subsequent chapters, it may be useful to describe its basis and operation. Open education has grown out of practical experience rather than philosophical or scientific foundations. Although writings on open education occasionally mention Freud and Piaget, it is not a theory or system of education, but a related set of ideas and methods. Content analysis of major writings on open education reveals that the movement resonates with the educational thoughts of Rousseau in France and Tolstoy in Russia and with the methods used in the one-room prairie schoolhouse in America in the nineteenth century and by some progressives during the 1920s and 1930s.[23] Open education rests philosophically on phenomenology rather than elementism and is antipathetic to a line of mainstream Anglo-American educators who classify the curriculum into subjects and group learners by ability and view knowledge as represented authoritatively by the teacher or in prescribed vicarious materials of instruction.[24] Open education is more consonant with continental structural psychology and with some parts of American clinical and developmental psychologies than with the psychologies most influential in twentieth-century American education—connectionism, behaviorism, and psychometrics.

Open education is difficult to characterize in the manner that behavioral scientists are accustomed to use in putting concepts into operation, for it is founded upon contingency and uniqueness, with each student, teacher, and event regarded as unique. The feelings and behavior of the teacher in open education cannot be easily categorized because her guiding principle is to respond as sensitively and reflectively as possible to the unique child at precise moments in the temporal stream and situational gestalt of her interaction with him. Also implicit in the approach is a view of the child as a significant decision maker in determining the direction, scope, means, and pace of his education. Open educators hold that the teacher and the child, in complementary roles, should together fashion the child's school experience. Thus, open education differs from teacher-centered, child-centered, and programmed, textbook, or other materials-centered approaches in that both the teacher and the child determine learning goals, materials, and activities.[25]

Recent research in England and United States reveals how these general ideas are carried out in the classroom.[26] The following points are some of those observed more frequently in open than in other classes. Diverse materials are supplied with little replication and no class sets. Children read "books" written by their classmates and use many materials brought in by their classmates. Children's activities, products, and ideas are abundant in the classroom. Children group themselves by their own choices and talk and move about freely. The teacher strives for an "integrated day" and avoids dividing instruction into discrete subjects or units and avoids grouping children by categories of ability, achievement, sex, or age. Before suggesting any extension or redirection of activity, the teacher gives diagnostic attention to the particular child and the evolution of his particular activity. The teacher keeps a longitudinal collection of each child's work to assess his development and views evaluation as developmental information to guide instruction. As one might infer from these practices, open educators are strongly opposed to multiple-choice achievement tests for evaluating either children or open programs. They resist elementist behavioristic evaluation, but try to encourage examination of the child's activities and products, longitudinal case studies, naturalistic observation, introspection by participating observers, and other continental methods of research.

The greatest threat to open education is not from either kind of research but from its woolly-minded enthusiasts who believe that removing classroom walls or permitting the child to plan his activities on his own produces open education. Open education (third cell, Table 1-6) has little to do with architecture, and it contrasts sharply with laissez-faire and free school methods (first cell), since the teacher's role in guiding each child is viewed as both active and demanding. Leading advocates of open education have tried to keep the movement true to their ideals and methods without imposing an othodoxy. They are distressed by practitioners (and even scholars) who confuse their ideas with educational permissiveness; indeed, they appear to prefer traditional British and American education (fourth cell) to the mingling of open education with laissez-faire or materials-centered approaches (third and second cells). Open educators might, on the other hand, promote the clarity and distinctiveness of the movement by further description of their theories of instruction and assumptions about child development in both analytic and operational terms. Some possible starting points have been specified in this section: open education might be best characterized as the multivalent (Figure 1-2) with joint teacher-student control and the occasional use of multimodal, enrichment, and acceleration. A variety of other characterizations are given in a recent work edited by Spodek and Walberg.[27]

Conclusion

This essay presents certain problems of formulating educational goals and setting their priorities and of deriving the scope, depth, and sequence of curriculum content. These problems of value are at least as important and difficult as the more technical issues of psychology and instruction treated here. And, as we have seen, techniques cannot be sharply separated from values; they are, in practice, based not only on presuppositions about the nature of the child, his development, and the learning process but also on assumptions about goals and the nature of knowledge. A means of instruction, thought to be neutral or adaptable to any goal, may in fact entail unrecognized learning consequences with far-reaching, long-term educational significance. Thus psychologists and others interested in the theory and practice of instruction must determine both the extent to which different means attain a given educational goal and the unintended consequences of different means. The determination of unintended consequences is less obvious and simple but no less critical for society and the individual.

Notes

1. For a number of points of view, see *Rethinking Educational Equality*, ed. Andrew T. Kopan and Herbert J. Walberg (Berkeley, Calif.: McCutchan Publishing Corp., 1974).

2. Klaus F. Riegel, "Influence of Economic and Political Ideologies on the Development of Developmental Psychology," *Psychological Bulletin* 78 (February 1972): 129-41.

3. Edwin G. Boring, *A History of Experimental Psychology* (New York: Appleton-Century-Crofts, 1957).

4. Roger G. Barker and Herbert F. Wright, *One Boy's Day* (New York: Harper-Row, 1951); Benjamin S. Bloom, *Stability and Change in Human Characteristics* (New York: John Wiley & Sons, 1964); Egon Brunswik, *Systematic and Representative Design of Psychological Experiments* (Berkeley, Calif.: University of California Press, 1949); Lee J. Cronbach, "The Two Disciplines of Scientific Psychology," *American Psychologist* 12 (1957): 671-84; Lee J. Cronbach and Richard E. Snow, *Instructional Methods and Aptitudes* (New York: Appleton-Century-Crofts, 1974); Henry A. Murray, *Explorations in Personality* (New York: Oxford University Press, 1938); Jean Piaget, *Science of Education and the Psychology of the Child* (New York: Orion Press, 1968); Herbert J. Walberg, "Models for Optimizing and Individualizing School Learning," *Interchange* 2 (1971): 15-27; Herbert J. Walberg and Kevin Marjoribanks, "Differential Mental Abilities and Home Environment: A Canonical Analysis," *Developmental Psychology* 9 (1973): 363-85; Herbert J. Walberg and Kevin Marjoribanks, "Home Environment and Cognitive Development: Toward a Generalized Causal Analysis," in *Education and Environment*, ed. Kevin Marjoribanks (London: National Foundation for Educational Research, 1974).

5. Cronbach, *op. cit.*

6. Herbert J. Walberg, "Optimization Reconsidered," in *Evaluating Educational Performance: A Source Book of Methods, Instruments, and Examples*, ed. Herbert J. Walberg (Berkeley, Calif.: McCutchan Publishing Corp., 1974), 375-95.

7. Boring, *op. cit.*

8. W. W. Bartley, *Wittgenstein* (New York: Lippincott, 1973).

9. For a more extensive analysis, see Boring, *op. cit.*; Richard W. Coan, "Dimensions of Psychological Theory," *American Psychologist* 23 (October 1968): 715-22; Cronbach, *op. cit.*; William D. Hitt, "Two Models of Man," *American Psychologist* 24 (July 1969): 651-58; Richard E. Snow, "Theory Construction for Research on Teaching," in *Second Handbook of Research on Teaching*, ed. Robert M. W. Travers (Chicago: Rand-McNally, 1973), 77-112; Walberg, "Models for Optimizing and Individualizing School Learning"; Herbert J. Walberg, "Overview of Social Psychology," in *Social Science Content for Preparing Educational Leaders*, ed. Jack Culbertson *et al.* (Columbus, Ohio: Merrill Press, 1973), 61-86.

10. Walberg, "Models for Optimizing and Individualizing School Learning."

11. Ruth Strang, *Behavior and Background of Students in College and Secondary School* (New York: Harper and Row, 1937).

12. John M. Stephens, *The Process of Schooling: A Psychological Examina-tion* (New York: Holt, Rinehart and Winston, 1968).

13. Thomas A. Romberg and John G. Harvey, *Developing Mathematical Processes: Background and Projections* (Madison, Wis.: Wisconsin Research and Development Center for Cognitive Learning, 1969).

14. Wayne Otto, *The Wisconsin Prototypic System of Reading Skill Develop-ment: An Interim Report* (Madison, Wis.: Wisconsin Research and Development Center for Cognitive Learning, 1969).

15. Miriam Bar-Yam, "The Interaction of Student Characteristics with Instructional Strategies: A Study of Students' Performance and Attitudes in an Innovative High School Course," unpublished Ph.D. dissertation, Harvard University, 1969.

16. Cronbach and Snow, *op. cit.*

17. Arnold B. Grobman, *The Changing Classroom: The Role of the Biological Sciences Curriculum Study* (Garden City, N.Y.: Doubleday, 1969).

18. Described in Wayne W. Welch and Herbert J. Walberg, "A National Experi-ment in Curriculum Evaluation," *American Educational Research Journal* 9 (Summer 1972): 373-84.

19. Jeffrey Rackham, "Technology, Control, and Organization," in *Industrial Society*, ed. Dennis Pym (Baltimore: Penguin Books, 1968), 335-53.

20. Walberg, "Models for Optimizing and Individualizing School Learning."

21. Max Weber, *The Theory of Social and Economic Organization* (New York: Oxford University Press, 1949).

22. Alfred N. Whitehead, *The Aims of Education* (New York: Macmillan, 1929), 96.

23. Herbert J. Walberg and Susan C. Thomas, *Characteristics of Open Educa-tion: Toward an Operational Definition* (Newton, Mass.: TDR Associates, 1971).

24. Walberg, "Models for Optimizing and Individualizing School Learning."

25. Anne M. Bussis and Edward A. Chittenden, *Analyses of an Approach to Open Education* (Princeton, N.J.: Educational Testing Services, 1970); Walberg and Thomas, *op. cit.*

26. Herbert J. Walberg and Susan C. Thomas, "Open Education: An Opera-tional Definition and Validation in Great Britain and United States," *American Educational Research Journal* 9 (Spring 1972): 197-208.

27. Bernard Spodek and Herbert J. Walberg, *Studies in Open Education* (New York: Agathon Press, 1974).

2. Instructional Design
for Individualization

Harriet Talmage

An instructional design model for developing and implementing systems of individualized education should provide a framework that can accommodate a variety of individualized programs; it should also account for the variations found in the general models of individualization discussed in the preceding chapter. The purpose of this chapter is to present one such model for instructional design, to illustrate how it can be used in guiding a program designer's decisions, and to assist the reader in identifying the design characteristics of the three systems of individualized education discussed in Chapters 3, 4, and 5.

Tyler has developed one model for curriculum and instructional design.[1] His rationale for developing curricula has assisted curriculum and instructional designers over the past two decades in identifying and conceptualizing the relevant design constructs. Tyler raised four questions from which the design constructs are derived:

1. What educational purposes should the school seek to attain?
2. How can learning experiences be selected which are likely to be useful in attaining these objectives?
3. How can learning experiences be organized for effective instruction?
4. How can the effectiveness of learning experiences be evaluated?[2]

In effect, the first question identifies the construct "objectives"; the second question considers the construct "modes of transaction"; the third question refers to organization of learning experiences; and the fourth question defines the construct "evaluation."

Recent interest in evaluation of instructional technology and instructional materials has led to an examination of designs of instruction.[3] A study of these designs tends to validate Tyler's constructs. Those concerned with instructional design have modified the constructs to accommodate what is presently understood about learning and about the design of instructional materials. Glaser, for example, adds the construct "entry behavior" to his design. Tyler, on the other hand, uses the information about the learner's entry behavior to select appropriate objectives for a given group of learners. Eash is concerned with the organization or the content of the learning materials. Whether a new construct, entry behavior, is added to the four constructs outlined by Tyler, or whether the emphasis in the construct "organization" is on the learning experience or on the arrangements of content that support selected learning experiences, the Tyler rationale provides in the main a basis for discussing instructional design.

In explicating a design for individualization, fifteen components of instruction are identified.[4] These components appear to fall within one or another of the four constructs. Developers of individualized instructional systems, programs, or materials either explicitly or implicitly account for these components in their product. Components have a range of characteristics from which the developers must choose, such as open to closed, fixed to variable, structured to nonstructured, linear to random. The model or combination of models for individualized instruction determines the specific characteristics of the components to be selected in an individualized instructional system. If, for example, variable learning outcomes are a feature of a given model, the pertinent characteristic of the component in each construct should provide for variable learning outcomes. Thus an organizational framework for discussing instructional design emerges: the design constructs; the design components; and the characteristics of the components.

Table 2-1 classifies the fifteen components of instruction under the related constructs. These are explained in the following section, and the range of decisions for selecting the characteristics of the components is discussed.

Table 2-1
Classification of components under the
instructional design constructs

ENTRY BEHAVIOR OF THE TARGET POPULATION

I. *Objectives*
  a. General program objectives
  b. Specific learning objectives
II. *Organization*[a]
  a. Structure of content
  b. Sequence of organization
  c. Scope of organization
  d. Branching
  e. Recycling
III. *Modes of transaction*
  a. Teacher-learner roles
  b. Management of learning environment
  c. Grouping
  d. Modes of presentation
  e. Time and pacing
  f. Learning activities
IV. *Evaluation*
  a. Instructional components
    1. Normative-criterion-referenced
    2. Teacher-learner-referenced
  b. Program evaluation
    1. Evaluation of program design
    2. Evaluation of performance of learner
    3. Evaluation of implementation process
    4. Evaluation of cost-effectiveness

---

[a]The order of presenting the constructs, organization, and modes of transaction has been reversed from the order in the Tyler rationale. Although that rationale places the methodological or transactional decisions prior to organization of learning experiences, I feel that organization of the content for developing individualized instructional delivery systems needs to precede methodological considerations. Decisions about what is to be learned will determine how the content will be delivered or the way the learner interacts with materials, his environment, and other persons. For large individualized instructional delivery systems, selection and ordering of the content are determined by the entry behavior of the target population, the general program objectives, and the outcome goals. These factors in turn determine the transactional decisions that facilitate learning. This does not preclude subsequent modifications in the components of organization.

Entry Behavior of the Target Population

The characteristics of the target population will help to shape the general program objectives and the specific learning objectives. Developers need to be concerned with such questions as: Are the learners highly motivated or reluctant to learn? Do they show unusual aptitude in certain areas of study, or are they having difficulty mastering quantitative or qualitative concepts? Do the learners represent a heterogeneous or a homogeneous group with respect to ability? Do they come with particular learning biases that have been demonstrated to affect learning? The cognitive, affective, and psychomotor attributes of the learners should be one source of educational objectives. Only after the entry behavior of the target population is identified can the program designer select the appropriate objectives and specify the learning outcomes.

Objectives as a Design Construct

The general program objectives refer to the goals and underlying philosophy of individualization. Is the intent of individualized instruction to encourage positive attitudes toward learning by reducing competition? Is the intent to foster self-direction by providing the learner with alternative learning objectives? Or is the intent to match the learner with the presentation mode that appears to fit his learning style? The general objectives are formulated to reflect the entry behavior of the target population. Other sources of the program objectives are derived from the subject under study, the psychology of learning, and the role attributed to society and to the learner.

Specific learning objectives operationalize the general program objectives by specifying the intended outcome behaviors. If the general objective, as an example, is to foster self-directed learning, the specific objectives should specify the types of behavior that are associated with self-direction. Thus, among the specific objectives would be the following: The student will choose a learning activity from among several alternative activities. He will monitor his own time. He will submit alternative objectives he proposes to pursue. He will evaluate his own performance based on established criteria. He will take responsibility for returning materials to their designated places. He will prepare an appropriate list of alternative learning activities for attaining a given objective and use these as his learning activities. To ensure attainment of self-directed learning, the characteristics of the other design constructs must be selected to support the specific learning objectives.

Depending on the general objectives, intended outcome behaviors are fixed or variable; some types of individualized programs are designed with fixed outcomes, others with variable outcomes. Learning to thread a sewing machine needle has a fixed outcome. Threading the needle is the outcome of the intended learning. Making a blouse may have a fixed or a variable outcome. While the intended learning is making a blouse, the outcomes can differ from learner to learner if each learner is given the freedom to vary the pattern. It would seem consistent with the meaning of self-direction if the intended outcome behaviors, in this case, were variable.

Fixed and variable outcomes can be measured in terms of the degree of learning. Specific learning objectives identify the degree of learning that will constitute acceptable performance or mastery of a set of specific objectives. Threading a sewing machine needle will, for example, be measured in terms of a given standard of time, dexterity, and accuracy. In "mastery learning" the degree of learning to be regarded as mastery is specified in advance.[5] Where individualized instructional programs have fixed outcomes, the criterion for mastery of the specific objective is identified; the student may, for example, be expected to attain 80 percent of the specific objectives as an indication of mastery, that is, thread a sewing machine needle expeditiously 80 percent of the time. Programs with variable outcome behaviors may or may not incorporate a criterion for mastery. Some programs with variable outcomes may include a criterion for mastery in each specific learning objective, but not specify the number of objectives in the program to be mastered. Other individualized programs may not indicate any criterion for mastery. A well-designed individualized program should include specific learning objectives that specify the type of outcome behaviors consonant with the general program objectives and the entry behavior of the target population.

Organization as a Design Construct

Content is the milieu for engaging the learner in activities leading to the intended outcome behaviors. Decisions concerning organization of the content draw on a number of sources, including the structure of the content, the entry behavior and program objectives, a logical order dictated by the nature of an academic discipline, and learning theory that suggests an optimum sequence.

Content must be organized in ways that make the learning experiences meaningful and that reinforce the experiences for successful learning. The selection and arrangement of the content assume an identifiable structure when a body of unassorted information is given a conceptual focus. If the study of science is conceptualized as a process, then the materials selected for inclusion in the program may differ from materials included in a science program stressing acquisition of information, or a mathematical, historical, or topical approach. Although portions of the content may be similar in these science programs, the arrangement of the content will differ.

The entry behavior of the target population and the general program objectives are also guides for selecting and ordering the content. If, for example, the learners can be described as having well-developed verbal skills at entry and a general program objective emphasizes self-direction, the content should be selected and organized so as to draw upon the verbal skills as well as to facilitate self-direction. Content that is linearly sequenced in short discrete steps may impede acquisition of self-directed learning. An instructional designer also selects and arranges the content to reflect the logical order of a discipline and the sequencing of requisite skills for subsequent learning. Should addition precede the learning of multiplication? Is it better for primary students to examine their immediate environment first or to experience the larger community first and then relate this back to their immediate environment?

Despite the many sources the designer can draw upon, in many instances the content of individualized programs is selected and arranged with no discernible structure other than a parochial view of individualization, such as self-pacing.

Once the structure of the content is defined, the designer selects the appropriate characteristics of the sequence and scope components. Is the sequence to have an initial fixed entry point for proceeding through the material linearly, or can the learner enter the program randomly, through differentiated entry points, and then proceed through the materials linearly? The content can also be arranged in a nonlinear pattern, so that each increment of learning is not predicated on skills or knowledge developed in the preceding increment. The designer must go back to his initial general program objectives on individualized learning to select the sequence that reinforces those objectives. As an example, in an individualized instructional program designed to foster self-directed learning the designer must determine what is meant by self-directed learning in the specific objectives before deciding on the sequential arrangement of the content.

The scope of the content refers to its breadth and depth. Breadth is that aspect of scope that stretches over a wide range of topics, while depth refers to the extent to which the content covers a single topic or concept. In organizing the content for individualized instruction, the designer makes decisions on how much and in what detail the content is to be studied. A survey of American history in the middle grades may reflect a wide breadth of content coverage, while any single topic may lack in-depth coverage. The content structure, objectives of the individualized program, and the learner's interest and ability determine the scope. For individualized programs, the scope can be arranged for fixed or flexible coverage by the learner. Depending again on the entry behavior, general program objectives, and the characteristics of the sequence, the learner may be required to proceed through all the materials or only as far as his interest and ability will carry him.

Branching and recycling are two other components of the construct organization, which must be decided upon in an individualized program once the characteristics of the scope and sequence components are determined. Branching provides alternative routes for achieving the intended learning. Multiple routes used in individualized programs are based on the learning style of the individual, his interests, or specific problems the learner may encounter as determined by his entry behavior. If the time for completing an individualized program is fixed, instructional designers must give greater attention to determining the characteristics of the branching component than if the completion time requirements are variable. With fixed-time individualized programs, the organization of the content should provide for the unused portion of the time of the learner who is faster paced.

The organization of individualized programs can offer other routes for achieving mastery when the learner fails to accomplish the objective through the prescribed sequence. This is called recycling. Engaging the learner in the learning activity through encounters with the content does not always ensure the attainment of the desired outcome. The content needs to be reordered to provide the learner with additional opportunity for learning. As an example, the content introduces an upper primary class to addition problems that require the operation of regrouping. Provision must be made for the student to have additional opportunities with this type of arithmetic operation should he meet with difficulty. Recycling could involve mere repetition, or a new set of similar problems (that is, modes of presentation such as tactile rather than audiovisual), or a different arrangement of pupils for instruction.

Designing an individualized program requires close attention to determination of the characteristics of the five components subsumed under organization of content. The characteristics of each component must support the objectives of the program, be consistent from component to component, and reinforce the program's general objectives.

Modes of Transaction as a Design Construct

The process of learning involves transactions between the learner and the instructional materials, the learner and the learning environment, the learner and his peers, and the learner and the teacher. The "modes of transaction" construct includes instructional components that affect the learning process. Selecting the appropriate characteristic of the components may necessitate some modification in the program's organization following validation studies. Like a well-tuned engine, these adjustments are required to reflect the peculiarities of each learner. A well-designed individualized program permits such adjustments.

Designers of individualized instructional programs have to account for six transactional components: teacher-learner roles; management of learning environment; grouping; modes of presentation; time and pacing; and learning activities. The model for an individualized instructional program determines the teacher-learner roles. The prescribed roles are supported by the organization of the content. The organization of a carefully structured, linearly sequenced program with a fixed entry point permits little or no deviation in the prescribed role of the teacher as far as making decisions about the organization of the content. Such a program may require the teacher to facilitate rather than actively to direct instruction. In other individualized programs the teacher is expected to guide the learners toward activities best suited to their interests or abilities; the teacher serves as a diagnostician and prescriber and plays an active role in selecting pertinent portions of the individualized program for the learner. Individualized programs may also dictate the teacher's role in dispensing rewards.

Different models for individualized instruction also have built-in roles for the learner. Under some designs the learner has an active decision-making role: he selects his materials and the other learners with whom he interacts, and he may determine how much of the program he will complete and how long it will take. In other designs, decisions made in the organization of the content and in the preselection of learning activities leave little in the hands of the teacher or the learner; if either were to assume roles other than those specified, violation could be done to the total design of the individualized program.

Who manages and maintains the learning environment is another important aspect of role definition. While management and maintenance are, however, functions of the designated roles of teachers or learners, these aspects can better be discussed under the learning environment.

The arrangement of the learning environment is either explicitly or implicitly identified in the design and is arranged and managed to support the general program objectives and to facilitate the roles prescribed for teachers and learners. The environment can take on different degrees of structure, from a totally open physical environment to a closed arrangement. The classroom can be viewed as a functioning social system. To provide for this view of the classroom, the arrangement and management of the learning environment will differ radically from a classroom viewed as a space to be portioned off to support uninterrupted interaction between the individual learner and the prescribed learning activity. The design may call for different degrees of movement and tolerate varying levels of noise. The arrangement of the physical equipment and spacing of the materials can create a cluttered and noisy environment or an ordered and calm one. Displays may affect a classroom atmosphere:

instructional materials that are openly displayed in an inviting arrangement permit the learner to interact with the materials more than those materials kept locked in cabinets and only available on request.

Individualized instruction built around programmed learning materials requires that space be arranged to enhance the interaction of the learner with the materials and to minimize interference or disturbance from others who share the larger classroom environment. A program based on a model for individualization that provides multiple-entry routes and branching options and objectives that encourage self-directed learning will, on the other hand, require an open environment that permits free access to materials, variations in grouping arrangements, movement, and responsibility of the learner for maintaining the environment.

Practitioners' understanding of individualized instruction has come a long way since the resurgence of interest in individualization. During the 1960s individualized instruction was associated with teaching machines and programmed texts and conjured up images of a single learner alone in timeless space, facing a panel board with several control knobs, and responding to bits of stimuli that had been previously tested and sequenced in a manner that ensured successful learning. To break from this image of individualization, the term "personalized learning" was coined. Although it is seldom operationally defined, its intent is to convey to program designers that individualized learning should be more than a single learner interacting with a single book or piece of equipment. The role of socialization in education should not be sacrificed; nor should individualized learning be so designed as to preclude the learner's being a decision maker in his own learning. The concept of individualized instruction does not, of course, eliminate the possibility that learning can take place in groups. Many grouping patterns are, as a matter of fact, congenial to the concept of individualized instruction. Learning groups can be arranged in terms of size, interest, ability, socially supportive groups, and academically supportive groups. Different individualized instructional programs may use one or more grouping patterns. The individualized instructional delivery systems described in the following three chapters illustrate variations of grouping patterns.

Designers of individualized instructional programs are concerned with the modes of communication used in presenting the learning stimuli. These modes of presentation encompass media, materials, and people. The usual media for communication in schools are visual, auditory, tactile, and/or some combination of them. Instructional materials (hardware and software) for an individualized program are selected to facilitate delivery of the messages communicated through the media. People as well as materials are sources for communicating stimuli. Some individualized programs require a single medium or one combination of media, while others require a variety of media, materials, and persons with whom the learner interacts. Instructional systems today may require many auxiliary personnel assisting the teacher or the learner as sources communicating learning stimuli; they include classroom clerical aides, instructional aides, master teachers, the learner's peers, advanced student helpers, student teachers, and community volunteers. Some individualized instructional programs are designed for maximum utilization of a variety of presentation modes; other programs keep the stimuli simple. There is evidence that different learners respond differentially to different modes of presentation. Some learners interact more effectively with stimuli presented visually than those presented orally, or with a single instructor rather than a host of dispensers of stimuli. Though, to date, research in the field cannot prescribe with certainty the ideal combination of modes of presentation that is most effective with a given individual learner, some decisions can nonetheless be made. Written stimuli cannot, of course, be as effective with nonreaders as some other mode of presentation. Thus, the designer of individualized instructional programs must take into consideration the entry behavior of the target population in selecting the modes of presentation.

In the past, time and pacing were major concerns of the designers of individualized programs. Time was considered the critical component in achieving mastery learning. Mastery of the intended outcome behaviors was seen as an individual process requiring a varying amount of time in which one was exposed to the materials and learning activities. Hence, programs were thought to be individualized to the extent that they provided for differential exposure in learning time. For other programs, pacing was the critical variable. Each learner was said to be governed by his own internal time clock and to move through the learning activities at a different pace; he should, thus, be able to complete the entire program at the pace best suited to him. More recent individualized programs give high priority to socialization and may feel it advantageous to hold groups of learners together yet provide for differential pacing. It is necessary for these programs to provide a branching component in the design.

Precisely how learning takes place is still a subject of discussion, but that it occurs only through response to stimuli is axiomatic. The learning activity as an instructional component is a subject of utmost concern to the designer. He must consider such questions as: To what extent should the learning stimuli be ordered and in what manner? What kinds of responses can be elicited by which learning activity? At what level of learning does the learner respond in carrying out the learning activity? Are the learning activities held constant (that is, all learners participate in the same prescribed learning activities), and time and pacing allowed to vary? Is a range of learning activities to be provided in the individualized program to accommodate different learners as identified by the entry behavior? Do different learning activities lead to the same goals? Can learners engage in the same learning activities and arrive at different outcome behaviors?

If the learning activities are carefully developed, the learner has an opportunity to engage in different levels of the thought process. Learning activities can encourage discovery of generalizations, analysis of relationships, interpretation of and extrapolation from given facts, rules, and principles in addition to the acquisition of basic factual information and verbal and social skills. If the designer is developing a self-directed individualized program, the role of the learner and the learning activities must foster self-direction.

Regardless of the type of individualized program, the six components of the mode of transaction construct must be provided in a manner that is consistent within the construct as well as with the characteristics of the other design components.

Evaluation as a Design Construct

Evaluation as a construct is concerned with two components: provision for measurement of performance, and the role and purpose of evaluation in the program. Beyond evaluating the instructional components, one must also evaluate the totality of the instructional program. It is, further, essential to give attention to the larger question of evaluation of the program design. The distinction between these two focuses of evaluation can be noted in Table 2-1.

Components of Evaluation

Two components are subsumed under evaluation as a design construct. The first is concerned with a measurement of performance, that is, with providing a yardstick for determining the achievement of the specific learning objectives. Is achievement criterion referenced or normative referenced?[6] Criterion references predicate achievement on a predetermined mastery level. For example, the criterion for attainment of a specific objective, such as subtracting two-digit numbers, may be set at 90 percent accuracy. Successful performance can only be achieved by the learner who reaches this level. Because this form of measurement places learners in only two categories (mastery achieved or mastery not achieved), it tends to reduce competitiveness. Another form of criterion-referenced measurement is the gain score (measuring achievement in terms of the individual's pre- and postscore progress). Normative-referenced measurements, on the other hand, compare a learner's performance with a given norming group. Compared to different norming groups, 90 percent accuracy may or may not be considered an acceptable level of achievement.

The second component of evaluation deals with the role of evaluation and the purpose of evaluation information as feedback to the program. Are the evaluation suggestions and materials provided in the individualized program teacher centered and for teacher information or learner centered and for learner information? Where the general program objectives in self-directed learning include active participation by learners, they should monitor their own progress and discover how to use the evaluation information to make decisions about their own learning. Such a system should provide built-in materials for self-evaluation and help the learner determine his own strengths and weaknesses.

Program Design Evaluation

Evaluation of an individualized instructional delivery system is a vehicle for making modifications in the design on the basis of accumulated data and for making value judgments about the system.

These forms of evaluation are termed formative and summative, respectively. Related to them are product and process evaluation which focus on procedures and results. Instructional programs, however, should be examined from a somewhat different set of evaluation referents as is suggested by the following questions: Are the characteristics of the instructional components consistent within each construct and across constructs? Can the learner attain the general and specific objectives, given the program's organization and modes of transaction? As it is designed, can the program be implemented in the school? Does the design provide a cost-effective individualized instructional delivery system? Each of the four referents (design consistency evaluation, learner validation evaluation, implementation evaluation, and cost-effectiveness evaluation) call into examination the fifteen instructional components. No individualized instructional delivery system should be disseminated on a large scale without conducting learner validation studies as a means of collecting data to determine whether the characteristics of the instructional components were selected appropriately, and field-testing the system to determine whether it can be implemented, under what conditions, and at what cost.

How the individualized instructional components are provided for in the overall design is not an issue concerning values. An individualized program that allows the learner multiple or random entry points is no better or worse than a program with a single entry point. Decisions are dependent on the entry behavior of the target group and the general program objectives. Individualized programs must fit the characteristics of individual learners. Too often designers of individualized programs seem to forget that no one program can be suitable for all individuals. Or, in the designer's zeal to have the individualized program reach a wider audience, the components may be selected inconsistently.

Emerging Instructional Designs: Selecting Appropriate Characteristics of the Individualized Instructional Components

A descriptive profile of the individualized instructional delivery systems emerges from the way the characteristics of the components are provided for in the system. The following pages illustrate the variety of programs that can emerge when programs are designed from models for individualized instruction or from general program objectives as points of departure for selecting the components' characteristics.

Using selected models discussed in Chapter 1, Table 2-2 illustrates the design profiles that emerge when components' characteristics are chosen in a manner consistent with the model. Making the correct decision concerning the appropriate component characteristics for the selection model, the hierarchical model, and the multivalent model is dependent on the predominant features of each model. The salient feature related to individualization in the selection model is a specific target group possessing narrowly defined entry behaviors, such as, for example, high achievers or children with hearing disability. Once the target population is selected, the other instructional components generally appear to mirror the design of most traditional programs, that is, fixed outcomes, fixed entry points, fixed time and pacing, limited decision-making role for the learner, large-group instruction, and normative-referenced evaluation. The predominant features of individualization in the hierarchical model are variable pacing, which permits each learner to control his pace, peer or individual grouping, variable entry points, and criterion-referenced evaluation of the learner's performance. The other design components may assume a number of characteristics as long as they are compatible with the model's salient features. The outstanding feature of individualization in the multivalent model is the assignment of a larger range of decisions to the learners than in the other two models, which is evidenced in the profile of the model shown in Table 2-2. The learner has control over his pacing, is permitted variable outcome behaviors, may make a choice of sequence with variable entry, can select learning activities utilizing a variety of presentation modes, and has opportunity for self-evaluation. The instructional systems that emerge from the models have characteristics that are effective in given situations; none of the systems would be most effective in all situations.

Designers do not necessarily work from a given model for individualized instruction; in many instances they proceed from a set of general program objectives that only indirectly suggest certain salient features of a single model or combination of models. Table 2-3 illustrates two design profiles that emerge when the characteristics of the components are selected in accordance with the general objectives. In

Table 2-2
Characteristics of individualized instructional components of three models for individualized instruction

Design constructs and instructional components	Selection model	Hierarchical model	Multivalent model
I. Objectives			
a. Entry behavior	Homogeneous target group on a given learner characteristic.	Heterogeneous target group.	Heterogeneous target group.
b. General program objectives	To enhance successful completion of the program of study as prescribed for a given target group.	To accommodate a program of study as differences in time individuals need to complete it.	To provide different learning opportunities based on individual characteristics of the learners.
c. Specific learning objectives	Fixed outcome behavior.	Fixed outcome behavior.	Variable outcome behavior.
II. Organization			
a. Structure of content	Single structure varies from design to design.	Single structure varies from design to design. Outcome goals build on the understandings and skills acquired in the previous unit of instruction.	Multiple structures can be accommodated in a linear sequence of instruction.
b. Sequence	Fixed sequence with single fixed entry point for all learners.	Fixed sequence with variable entry points that depend on the entry behavior of each learner.	Multiple sequence; after initial selection of sequence, learner pursues a fixed sequence.
c. Scope	Depth and breadth vary from program to program.	Depth sufficient for every learner to master the outcome goals.	Depth and breadth dependent on the nature of the sequence.
d. Branching	Usually no provision for branching.	Variable entry points can be viewed as a form of branching; sometimes additional provisions for branching.	Multiple sequence can be viewed as a form of branching; additional provisions for branching.
e. Recycling	Usually no provision for recycling except repetition of the sequence.	Repetition of the unit of instruction or provision for recycling can be incorporated in the model.	Repetition of the unit of instruction or provision for recycling can be incorporated in the model.

III. Modes of transaction			
a. Teacher-learner roles (t-l role)	Roles usually defined by the program with limited or no t-l role as input to the program.	T-l decision-making options usually limited and defined; some learner responsibility for monitoring his own time.	T-l decision-making options can be provisioned to permit a range of teacher or learner decisions.
b. Management of learning environment	Usually highly structured.	Structured with accommodation for movement and free access to materials.	Structured or open depending on the general program objectives; where t-l roles include decision making, learning environment needs to be open.
c. Grouping	Total individual or total group instruction.	Individual; small groups sometimes called upon to reinforce a concept.	Variable groupings.
d. Modes of presentation	Prescribed by the program; may be limited or abundant.	Prescribed by the program; may be limited or may not be fixed; pacing is variable.	Usually varied modes.
e. Time and pacing	Both time and pacing are fixed.	Time may or may not be fixed; pacing is variable.	Time usually fixed; pacing for small groups and/or individual is variable.
f. Learning activities	Fixed by design; usually a single learning activity for each intended learning outcome.	Fixed by design; may offer a variety of learning activities or a single activity for each intended learning outcome.	Fixed by design, usually a variety of activities amenable to different grouping using many modes of presentation.
IV. Evaluation			
a. Normative-criterion-referenced	Normative-referenced.	Usually criterion-referenced based on predetermined mastery levels.	Characteristics of component are open; depends on general program objectives.
b. Teacher-learner-referenced	Teacher-referenced.	Amenable to teacher- or learner-referenced, depending on general program objectives.	Amenable to teacher- or learner-referenced, depending on general program objectives.

Table 2-3

Characteristics of individualized instructional constructs based on general program objectives of two hypothetical designs

Design constructs and instructional components	Hypothetical Design A	Hypothetical Design B
I. Objectives		
a. Entry behavior	Heterogeneous group of learners.	Heterogeneous group of learners.
b. General program objectives	As stated.	As stated.
c. Specific learning objectives	Fixed.	Variable.
II. Organization		
a. Structure of content	Learner presented with a pattern to be applied to computing $+$, $-$, $\div$, and x of fraction problems.	Content selected based on a wide range of situations for which fractions are applicable; business, science, etc. types of problems.
b. Sequence	Small discrete linear steps each building on a previous skill; variable entry point, sequence then fixed.	Random sequence, both for entry and for proceeding through the materials.
c. Scope	Limited to acquisition of computational skills with additional topics for faster paced learners.	Breadth of topics and examples to draw upon.
d. Branching	Provided for faster paced learners and alternative paths for learners who have not acquired the requisite computational skills.	Only indirectly provisioned; breadth of scope provides for branching opportunities.
e. Recycling	Provided in form of a different set of similar problems using the same general learning activities.	Recycling not considered necessary.

III. Modes of transaction		
a. Teacher-learner roles (t-l role)	Fixed by program.	Considerable decision-making responsibility given to the learner with the teacher arousing learner interest.
b. Management of learning environment	Closed.	Open.
c. Grouping	Fixed.	Variable.
d. Modes of presentation	Few; many times only a programmed text.	Abundant use of varying modes of presentation.
e. Time and pacing	Time fixed; pacing variable.	Variable time and pacing.
f. Learning activities	Fixed by design with a given activity for each specific objective.	Variety of learning activities suggested with provision for teacher and learner input.
IV. Evaluation		
a. Normative-criterion-referenced	Criterion-referenced.	Gain scores and criterion for measuring extent of specific objective attainment.
b. Teacher-learner-referenced	Teacher uses information to assist learner.	Self-evaluation a goal with teacher and learner planning further activities based on evaluation as feedback.

these illustrations, hypothetical Design A is based on a general program objective that emphasizes computational skills and variable pacing. Hypothetical Design B is based on a general program objective that emphasizes computational skills and variable pacing. Hypothetical Design B is based on a general program objective that emphasizes daily application and learner interests. Each focuses on different aspects of learning the concept of fractions and how that concept can best be learned. The two designs are summarized below.

The general program objective for Design A is to provide an efficient method for acquiring computational skills using fractions as well as to accommodate to differences in rates of learning.

The general program objective for Design B is to provide an understanding of the use of the concept "fraction" in a wide range of everyday situations and to accommodate to the interests of the learner.

The general objective for Design A is concerned with learning computational skills in addition, subtraction, multiplication, and division of fractions, using the deductive method for acquiring these skills. The learner is given a formula, a set of numbers to be used in the formula, and told to follow the prescribed steps. In division of fractions, the student is told to invert the divisor and proceed as in multiplication. This presumes, of course, that the student knows the rules for multiplying fractions. The approach will require a sequence employing discrete, linearly arranged steps, some attention to branching, fixed learning outcomes, variable pacing, and criterion-referenced evaluation.

The general objective for Design B is concerned with the application of fractions to everyday situations. The interests of the learners will guide the selection of situations. The teacher can help to stimulate interest in everyday situations requiring the application of fractions by posing relevant problems that call for solutions through problem-solving, inquiry, or discovery approaches. Computational skills will be regarded as a tool rather than as an end in themselves. The general objective will require a random entry sequence, a significant decision-making role for the learner, a teacher who is sensitive to the interests of the learners and can function as a problem generator when necessary, variable learning outcomes, and self-evaluation of progress by learners.

Design B is a more open design than Design A. It must be kept in mind, however, that Design B does not necessarily provide a better approach to individualization than Design A. Design A will prove more helpful to some learners, while others will learn more effectively by following Design B. Although neither hypothetical design takes on the profile of any one model for individualized instruction, each profile reflects characteristics that can be ascribed to one or more of the models.

Attention to instructional design may appear on the surface to be mechanistic and overly attentive to elementism in the Anglo-American traditions of developmental psychology. The profiles of instructional programs that emerge, however, take on a range of characteristics, some of which are not at variance with continental psychologies. The individualized educational systems discussed in the following three chapters select the design constructs and their components in ways that draw more heavily on Anglo-American than on continental tradition, although there are indications that a synthesis of these traditions is possible within the instructional design framework discussed above.

Notes

1. Ralph W. Tyler, *Basic Principles of Curriculum and Instruction* (Chicago: University of Chicago Press, 1949).

2. *Ibid.*, 1.

3. Robert Glaser, "The Design of Instruction," in *The Changing American School*, Sixty-fifth Yearbook of the National Society for the Study of Education, Part II (Chicago: University of Chicago Press, 1966), 215-42; Leslie J. Briggs, *Handbook of Procedures for the Design of Instruction*, Monograph No. 4 (Pittsburgh, Pa.: American Institutes for Research, 1970); and Maurice J. Eash, "Assessing Curriculum Materials: A Preliminary Instrument," *EPIE Educational Products Report* 2:5 (New York: Educational Products Information Exchange Institute, 1969): 18-24.

4. The fifteen components of instruction have been adapted for this discussion from Herbert J. Walberg, Harriet Talmage, Robert M. Rippey, and Maurice J. Eash, "Evaluating 'Individualized' Materials," *EPIE Educational Products Report* 46 (New York: Educational Products Information Exchange Institute, 1972): 12-19.

5. Benjamin S. Bloom, J. Thomas Hastings, George F. Madaus, *Handbook on Formative and Summative Evaluation of Student Learning* (New York: McGraw-Hill Book Company, 1971).

6. Robert Glaser, "Instructional Technology and the Measurement of Learning Outcomes: Some Questions," *American Psychologist* 18 (August 1963): 519-21.

3. IGE: An Alternative Form of Schooling

Herbert J. Klausmeier

Individually Guided Education (IGE), under continuous development by the Wisconsin Research and Development Center since 1964, has proven to be one effective alternative to age-graded, self-contained schooling at the elementary and middle school levels in a large number of school districts.[1] IGE is conceptualized as a comprehensive alternative system of schooling designed to produce higher educational achievements by providing effectively for differences among students in rate of learning, learning style, and other characteristics.[2]

The research reported in this chapter was conducted at the Wisconsin Research and Development Center for Cognitive Learning, which is supported in part as a research and development center by funds from the National Institute of Education, Department of Health, Education, and Welfare. The opinions expressed herein do not necessarily reflect the position or policy of the National Institute of Education, and no official endorsement by that agency should be inferred. (Center Contract No. NE-C-00-3--0065)
IGE acronyms are listed in the appendix at the end of the chapter.

Components of IGE

The seven major components of IGE are shown in Figure 3-1. Each component in itself is relatively complex, and together the seven components have far-reaching implications for instruction, administration, and home-school relations, among other functions. In what follows each component of IGE is explained more fully.[3]

The Multiunit School Organizational-Administrative Arrangements (MUS)

The MUS was designed to produce an environment in a school building that would facilitate instructional programming for the individual student and the introduction and practice of other components of IGE. The MUS is described by Klausmeier and Pellegrin as an invention of organizational arrangements that have emerged from a synthesis of theory and practice regarding instructional programming for the individual student, horizontal and vertical organization for instruction, role differentiation, shared decision making by groups, open communication among school personnel, and administrative and instructional accountability.[4]

Figure 3-2 shows the prototypic organization of the multiunit organization at the elementary school level (MUS-E). Variations from the prototype are made in terms of the number of students enrolled in the building, the availability of noncertified personnel, the size of the school district, and the like. The organizational hierarchy consists of interrelated groups at three distinct levels of operation: the instructional and research unit (I & R unit) at the classroom level; the instructional improvement committee (IIC) at the building level; and the systemwide policy committee (SPC) or a similar administrative arrangement at the school district level. Each of the first two levels is itself a hierarchical structure with clearly defined roles for personnel. Each of the three elements of the MUS-E, while taking the initiative for certain decisions, must secure information from each of the other elements. The building principal and the unit leaders, who serve at each of two levels as noted in Figure 3-2, provide the communication links among the three groups.

The I & R Unit

The nongraded I & R unit replaces the age-graded, self-contained

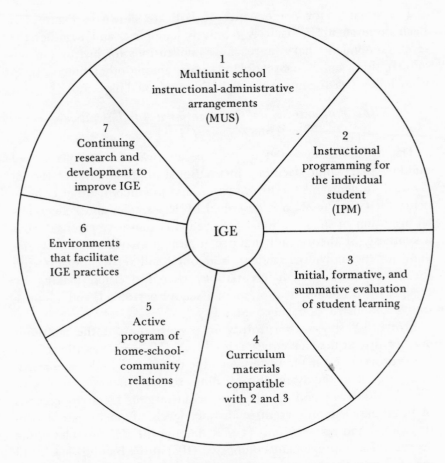

Figure 3-1

Major components of IGE—An alternative form of schooling (based on Herbert J. Klausmeier, Mary R. Quilling, Juanita S. Sorenson, Russell S. Way, and George R. Glasrud, *Individually Guided Education and the Multiunit Elementary School: Guidelines for Implementation* [Madison, Wis.: Wisconsin Research and Development Center for Cognitive Learning, 1971], Chapter 2)

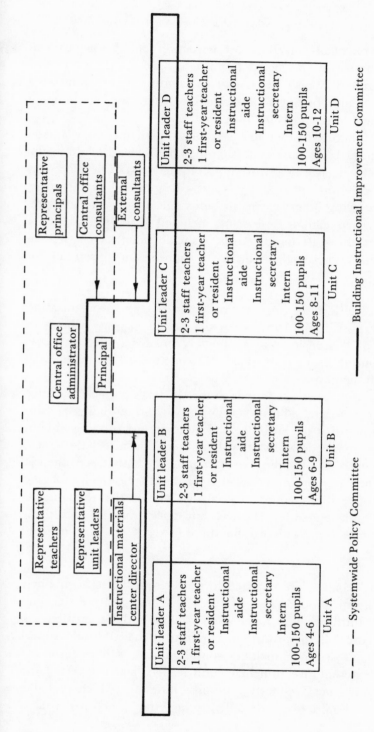

Figure 3-2

Prototype organization for a multiunit school of about 600 students (from Herbert J. Klausmeier, Richard G. Morrow, and James E. Walter, *Individually Guided Education in the Multiunit Elementary School: Guidelines for Implementation* [Madison, Wis.: Wisconsin Research and Development Center for Cognitive Learning, 1968], 18)

Text within figure:

Representative teachers

Representative unit leaders

Central office administrator

Representative principals

Central office consultants

External consultants

Instructional materials center director

Principal

Unit leader A
2-3 staff teachers
1 first-year teacher or resident
Instructional aide
Instructional secretary
Intern
100-150 pupils
Ages 4-6
Unit A

Unit leader B
2-3 staff teachers
1 first-year teacher or resident
Instructional aide
Instructional secretary
Intern
100-150 pupils
Ages 6-9
Unit B

Unit leader C
2-3 staff teachers
1 first-year teacher or resident
Instructional aide
Instructional secretary
Intern
100-150 pupils
Ages 8-11
Unit C

Unit leader D
2-3 staff teachers
1 first-year teacher or resident
Instructional aide
Instructional secretary
Intern
100-150 pupils
Ages 10-12
Unit D

– – – Systemwide Policy Committee

——— Building Instructional Improvement Committee

classroom form of organization for instruction and also departmentalized instruction at the elementary school level. In the prototype shown in Figure 3-2, each I & R unit has a unit leader, two or three staff teachers, one first-year or resident teacher, one instructional secretary, one intern, and 100-150 students.

The main function of each unit is to plan, carry out, and evaluate, as a hierarchical team, instructional programs for each child in the unit. Each unit engages in a continuous on-the-job staff development program. Some units plan and conduct research and development cooperatively with other agencies, and some are involved in preservice teacher education. Research is included in the title to reflect the fact that the staff must continuously do practical research in order to devise and evaluate an instructional program appropriate for each child.

The IIC

At the second level of organization is the IIC, a new organization that became possible in 1967 when the first elementary schools in three cities of Wisconsin were completely organized into units. As noted in Figure 3-2, the prototypic IIC is comprised of the building principal and the unit leaders.

The four main functions for which the IIC takes primary initiative are: stating the general educational objectives and outlining the educational program for the entire school building; interpreting and implementing systemwide and statewide policies that affect the educational program of the building; coordinating the activities of the I & R units to achieve continuity in all curriculum areas; and arranging for the use of facilities, time, material, and the like that the units do not manage independently. The IIC thus deals primarily with planning, decision making, and coordinating functions related to instruction.

The SPC

Substantial changes are required to move from the self-contained classroom organization to that of the I & R unit and the IIC. The SPC, at the third organizational level, facilitates this transition. As noted in Figure 3-2, the prototypic committee, chaired by the superintendent or his designee, includes consultants and other central office staff, representative principals, unit leaders, and teachers. Four decision-making and facilitative responsibilities for which the SPC takes primary initiative are: identifying the functions to be performed in each IGE school of the district; recruiting personnel for each IGE school and arranging for their in-service education; providing instructional materials; and disseminating information about IGE within the district and the community. A central office arrangement other than an SPC may be responsible for these functions; considerable flexibility is required since local school districts differ greatly in size and other characteristics.

Differentiated Roles

Unlike some differentiated staffing programs that create a complex hierarchy and call for a proliferation of new roles and titles for personnel, the multiunit organizational pattern establishes only one new position, that of unit leader or lead teacher. Basic changes are made, however, in the roles of the principal and teacher, and other roles are integrated into the unit, such as the teacher aide, instructional secretary, and intern. The multiunit pattern does not preclude the identification and establishment of other new, specialized roles such as those connected with instructional media or school-community relations. It does assume, however, that the unit leader and the unit staff, who work directly with the children and their parents, are the key individuals in the instructional system. The multiunit pattern also calls for a direct concentration of monetary resources and personnel of the school district in the daily program of instruction. In the discussion that follows, the key roles of the unit leader, staff teacher, and principal are described briefly.

The unit leader is a member of the IIC and a teacher in the unit. The role is that of a career teacher; it is clearly not administrative or supervisory. As a member of the IIC, the unit leader contributes to planning the entire program of the building, primarily by defining the program of his unit in relation to that of other units. As the leader of the unit, he plans and coordinates the efficient utilization of materials and resources; he performs liaison functions between the unit staff and the principal, consultants, parents, and others; and he instructs unit members, including beginning teachers and instructional aides. The unit leader teaches children from 50 to 80 percent of the time, the proportion depending upon the size of the unit and the amount of research and development and teacher education conducted in the unit. He is a model teacher of children and takes initiative in developing and trying out new materials and instructional procedures. In a recent study, Sheridan analyzed the expectations held for the unit leader's role by principals, teachers, and unit leaders themselves.[5] A factor analysis of the expectations revealed that the following major role categories are useful in describing this essential and emerging position in education: improving and maintaining intraunit relationships, managing and allocating resources, coordinating instructional activities, and initiating and enhancing extraorganizational relationships.

The role of the staff teacher is also changed in the multiunit school, where he participates in unit planning sessions, works with a large number of children in the unit, and performs more professional and less routine work. The collaborative planning, instruction, and evaluation called for in IGE demands specialization of tasks according to the capabilities and interests of each staff member. For example, the teacher who is strong in a curriculum area takes greater initiative in planning the unit activities in that area, in teaching other staff members, and in the actual teaching of children. Teachers may also be stronger or weaker in certain instructional groupings. One may be excellent in tutorial activities, another in small-group activities, and still another in large-group activities. Identifying or developing instructional materials, assessment tools and procedures, home-school procedures, and other specialized tasks are handled according to the individual characteristics of teachers. Each staff member takes greater initiative in the area of his strengths and interests, but he does not become completely specialized.

The role of the principal is changed in the multiunit school in that he assumes greater and more direct administrative responsibility for developing improved educational practices, managing the preservice and in-service teacher educational activities in his building, and administering research and development activities. He organizes and chairs the IIC—the mechanism and communication system through which he exercises administrative leadership. It is not assumed that the principal is an expert in any particular subject-matter field, in research design, or in teacher education. However, he utilizes the knowledge of his staff and consultants, delegates responsibility, and assists the IIC in arriving at decisions that can be implemented effectively.

A Model of Instructional Programming
for the Individual Student (IPM)

At the heart of IGE is the instructional programming model for the individual student (IPM) depicted in Figure 3-3.[6] It specifically takes into account each pupil's beginning level of performance, rate of progress, style of learning, motivational level, and other characteristics in the context of the educational program of the building. Instructional programming for the individual student is appropriately carried out in any area in the cognitive, psychomotor, or affective domains. It can be used with explicitly stated instructional objectives that specify mastery and also with expressive and general objectives that imply either activities to be carried out or progress to be made, rather than mastery of a particular objective.

IPM has been implemented most widely in schools that use recently developed materials for individualizing instruction, including the Wisconsin Design for Reading Skill Development (WDRSD)[7] and the system of Individually Guided Motivation (IGM)[8] developed at the Wisconsin R & D Center. The IPM may be applied to short, nonsequential, parallel instructional sequences, as is true for IGM, or to invariant sequences within various elements of a total instructional program, as is the case for WDRSD. Also, it may be implemented either through assessing students and then placing them in a preplanned instructional program, such as the WDRSD and Individually Prescribed Instruction (IPI)[9], or in assessing the students and then planning and carrying out a unique program for each student, such as in IGM. (WDRSD has explicitly stated objectives and assumes mastery learning; IGM has neither of these features.) The IPM sequence is illustrated by relating the six steps (outlined in Figure 3-3) to the Word Attack element of the WDRSD.

The first step involves the IIC's setting general educational objectives in Word Attack for the children of the building. A terminal objective for reading in a particular school might be: 90 percent of the children attain independence in Word Attack by age ten, 95 percent by age eleven, and 99 percent by age twelve. Initiative for setting this objective is taken by the IIC. Before the objective is set, of course, the unit leaders consult with the unit staffs. Establishing this schoolwide objective focuses attention of the unit staff on priorities, including the setting of instructional objectives for individual children and related instructional planning. If tutoring is possible in

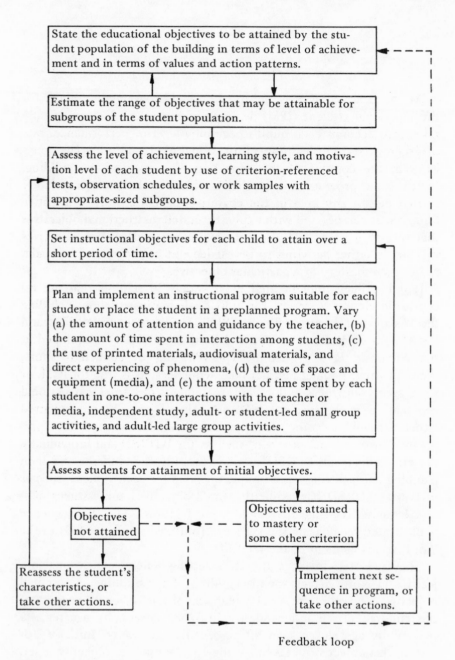

Feedback loop

Figure 3-3

Instructional programming model in IGE (from Klausmeier *et al.*, *Individually Guided Education and the Multiunit Elementary School*, 19)

only one curriculum area, for instance, it will probably be in Word Attack. Similarly, criteria and means will be formulated for assessing independence in Word Attack, and attainment of the objective, rather than age of the child or grade level in school, will determine when instruction in Word Attack skills ceases for an individual child.

The second step calls for identification by the I & R unit staff of a subset of specific instructional objectives that may be appropriate for a group of children. Only some of the forty-five Word Attack objectives, for example, are suitable for children in the early stage of reading.

The third step is the actual assessment of each child's level of development of skills, either by observing oral reading performances or by administering a group test that can be scored by a machine. Criterion-referenced tests have been developed and validated for use in assessing mastery of each instructional objective related to the various Word Attack skills. When the appropriate subset of objective-related tests is administered, the deficiencies in skills of each child are pinpointed, and instructional objectives for the individual child can be identified.

The fourth step involves setting instructional objectives for each child in the unit. Particular instructional objectives in the WDRSD recommended sequence in which the child is deficient become the child's instructional objectives.

The first phase of the fifth step involves planning an instructional program whereby the child attains his objectives. Reasonable cost of instruction and adequate progress of the pupil are provided for by proper grouping of the children for instruction and by utilizing the instructional staff according to the strengths of each member. Once general plans for the children are set, an individual teacher completes the detailed plan and carries it out for certain children, taking into account the suggestions of the other professionals in the unit. Each teacher generally instructs one or more groups of children who are working toward mastering the same skill. In each small group, materials, methods, use of time, and the like are matched to individual pupils with consideration given to their present level of skill development, rate of learning, preferred learning style, and other characteristics. Personal characteristics such as sociability, motivation, and emotional maturity are also given attention. To the extent that staff is available, individual tutoring and goal-setting conferences are provided for children who profit from them. Some schools have also developed other means of carrying out instruction at this point in the sequence.

In the sixth step of IPM pupils are assessed to determine their attainment of objectives. If the child has attained his instructional objective—that is, if he has met the 80 percent criterion level on the postassessment—he moves ahead in the sequence to the next objective. Assessment and related regrouping may occur every four weeks or less. If a child has failed to attain the objective, his readiness to attain it must be evaluated, as should other parts of the instructional programming sequence, as indicated in the feedback loop of Figure 3-3.

Thus, implementing the six steps of the IPM requires a schoolwide effort. In the IGE school, instructional programming is done by the teachers with assistance from the staffs of the building and the central office. Other types of assistance, however, should also be provided, among them criterion-referenced tests, rapid scoring of tests, more suitable instructional materials in the various curriculum areas, and computer management of the testing program and the related identification of alternative succeeding steps in the sequence. Computer management of IGE, however, is yet under development and not generally available.[10]

Model for the Evaluation of Students' Learning

An important element of the IPM involves evaluation of the student's learning characteristics, style of learning, and progress in learning. The sequence from measurement through evaluation and subsequent action may be depicted as follows:

Formulate instructional objective and set related criteria of attainment → measure → relate measurement to criteria → judge → act on judgment.[11]

The sequence is intended to be applied both to mastery learning and to other forms, such as in the affective domain, and also to either short, parallel instructional sequences or to completely sequenced programs extending through an entire level of schooling. Evaluative information related to either of these kinds of programs is secured at various points in time for specific purposes as shown in Table 3-1.

Table 3-1

Purposes and timing of evaluation of student learning in IGE

Focus of evaluation	Timing	Purpose
Short-term instructional sequence	Prior to starting a sequence (Initial Evaluation)	To arrange the instructional program for the individual student, or to place the student in a preplanned sequence.
	During an instructional sequence (Formative Evaluation)	To provide feedback information to the student to facilitate learning, and to the teacher to facilitate instruction.
	Upon completing a sequence (Summative Evaluation)	To determine whether the student has attained objective.
		To determine the effectiveness of instruction.
		To provide substantive basis for planning and action.
Complete educational program	Toward end of semester or year (Formative Evaluation)	To provide feedback to the student.
		To provide feedback to the teacher(s).
		To provide substantive basis for planning and action by the student and the teacher(s).
	At regular long-term intervals (Summative Evaluation)	To determine how well long-term educational objectives are being attained.
		To determine whether education is improving, deteriorating, remaining constant across time.
		To provide substantive basis for planning and action by school personnel and other educational policy makers.

Source: Based on Herbert J. Klausmeier and William L. Goodwin, *Learning and Human Abilities: Educational Psychology*, 4th ed. (New York: Harper and Row, in press).

As indicated in Table 3-1, evaluation of the student's learning characteristics and performances is aimed at providing information at three times: at the beginning of a unit of instruction, semester, or school year in order to set objectives for the student and to plan and arrange an instructional program appropriate for him; at various times throughout the instructional program to provide feedback to the student to facilitate his learning and to the teacher to arrange the best possible instruction; and at the end of a unit, semester, or school year so that a final indication of the student's progress is available and related decisions may be made.

Initial Evaluation

In instructional programming for the individual student, initial evaluation of each student is carried out before instruction starts. The evaluative information is used in planning either an appropriate instructional program for the student or in placing him in a pre-planned program, the latter being the more common practice.

When placing students in preplanned instructional programs, each student is assessed on the basis of a number of specific behaviors directly related to the program. The placement test, or battery of tests and observations, usually consists of a number of items keyed directly to the objectives of the program. In this connection, in the WDRSD, IPI, and in the curriculum areas as described for Project PLAN*, short achievement tests are given early in the year to place students in the proper unit of a sequential series of units.[12] Other information from accumulated observations may also be used in placing students or in planning programs for them.

Formative Evaluation to Facilitate Student Progress

Formative evaluation carried out during an instructional sequence involves assessing what the student has learned. This information is useful in identifying any problems that may need to be overcome by the student, the teacher, or both so that the student may continue to make progress. Students secure some evaluative information themselves; the skillful teacher assists them, particularly in identifying and overcoming problems.

Continuing systematic assessment of the student's progress is required in order to arrange appropriate instruction. For example, if an error in early placement has been made, it should be detected and corrected immediately. Or, a student may be correctly placed, but after initial success he may experience difficulty with the pacing of the instruction. Proper pacing requires assessing the student's acquisition of the content or skills, as well as his motivation. Evaluation so integrated within the instructional program provides corrective feedback. The student's progress is assessed mainly by use of work samples and observation of daily activities.

Summative Evaluation

In the case of mastery learning, evaluating mastery of objectives at the end of an instructional sequence proceeds in the same manner as described previously in connection with the initial evaluation of readiness. To summarize, criteria are set for determining attainment of the objectives, the student's achievement is measured, and his achievements are compared with the criteria. Decisions and actions follow. It is important, of course, that various alternatives be planned in advance since all students cannot be expected to attain mastery of an objective at the same time or through the same program; thus, appropriate and different actions may follow the evaluation.

Compatible Curriculum Materials

Many professors, scientists, and other personnel at the Wisconsin R & D Center have been developing curriculum materials that may be used in IGE and other schools. The principal groups of personnel and their curriculum areas merit attention inasmuch as the success of IGE depends heavily upon the availability of curriculum materials compatible with the IPM and the related evaluation of student learning.

The WDRSD describes essential reading skills and related instructional objectives and provides criterion-referenced tests that can be scored by machines for assessing children's mastery of the objectives. The program is organized into six areas: Word Attack, Study Skills, Comprehension, Self-directed Reading, Interpretive Skills, and Creative Skills. The first three areas include explicitly stated objectives and mastery learning; the last three incorporate expressive objectives and participation in suggested activities rather than mastery of skills or content. Except for the tests, the WDRSD materials are intended for use by teachers, not by children. Professor Wayne Otto and present and former scientists Robert Chester and Eunice Askov are the primary developers.

The Prereading Skills Program is designed to prevent reading failures by identifying and overcoming deficits in prereading skills at the preschool and kindergarten levels. Diagnostic tests have been developed for three visual skills (letter order, letter orientation, and word detail) and two auditory skills (sound matching and sound blending). Instructional packages to help children learn these skills include games, songs, and other activities. Informal assessment procedures and a handbook for teachers are also included. Professor Richard Venezky and Specialists Susan Pittelman and Marga Kamm are the primary developers.

Developing Mathematical Processes (DMP) is a comprehensive instructional and management program that integrates arithmetic, geometry, and probability and statistics. Based on an empirical analysis of how children learn mathematics, DMP incorporates an activity approach in a carefully sequenced program of mathematics instruction for children in the kindergarten through grade six. Geometry is integrated with the study of arithmetic by taking a measurement approach where children themselves generate the numbers they work with. Because they are constantly generating numerical data, children also study elementary probability and statistics as they organize and analyze these data. Professors Thomas Romberg and John Harvey and scientists James Moser and Mary Montgomery are the primary developers.

IGM is designed to increase children's interest in learning related to any curriculum area and also their self-direction. The in-service materials, including five films, a book to teach children to become tutors, and a book for instructional aides, explain and illustrate how principles of goal setting, modeling, feedback, reinforcement, and reasoning may be incorporated into various motivational-instructional procedures. The primary developers are the present author, former scientists Dorothy Frayer and Mary Quilling, and present scientist Jan Jeter.

Scientists Marvin Meissen and Jeter are developing an Environmental Education program in which the curriculum materials are designed to teach environmental concepts to elementary school children within a social studies context. Upper intermediate and lower intermediate instructional packages deal with such topics as population, pollution, land use, resource utilization, and the effects on the environment of technology and urbanization.

As perceived by the present author, IGE curriculum materials for schools, whether developed at the Wisconsin R & D Center or elsewhere, should incorporate four main attributes. First, the content incorporated in the material should be accurate and reliable. Second, the content should be learnable by the particular students for whom it is prepared. Third, the materials and related activities should be teachable. Fourth, the materials should be usable in terms of cost, attractiveness, and the amount of in-service teacher education required.

Procedures recommended to schools by Klausmeier and others for identifying and using instructional materials follow this general sequence: broad terminal educational objectives related to the major curriculum areas are formulated by a state, school district, or both.[13] A representative committee of teachers and administrators identifies possible printed and audiovisual instructional materials. From this larger list the staff of a building selects the items appropriate for each student to attain specified instructional objectives. Each building staff continuously recommends to the district committee the specific materials needed for the students attending the particular school.

Rossmiller, director of the Wisconsin R & D Center since October 1972, indicated that IGE schools should be able to choose among a variety of curriculum materials that they judge will best meet the needs of their students.[14] Materials produced by various regional educational laboratories, research and development centers, non-profit organizations, and profit-making agencies are used in IGE schools.

Active Program of Home-School-Community Relations

Fruth and Bowles identify the goals of an IGE home-school-community relations program.[15] They also formulated a strategy for implementing the program in terms of specific activities to maximize community participation, especially through interactions between parents and staff. Three general aims of the home-school-community relations program are: to make the IGE staff more aware of and responsive to the educational expectations and available resources of the community, parents, and children; to make the community, parents, and children more aware of and responsive to the nature of instructional programming for the individual student as implemented through IGE; and to identify and utilize ways and means of actively involving both staff and community in the early implementation and subsequent refinement of IGE in the educational program of a community.

Figure 3-4 indicates how Fruth and Bowles view home-school-community relations schematically at three interdependent levels. The first and outer level represents the larger community of the school district. In this regard, it is recognized that the community controls the schools through its willingness to expend its power and resources on programs that mirror its values and interests. If the values held by the community are communicated to the staff, and if the staff is responsive to these expectations, the community is likely to use its power and resources to support the values inherent in its instructional program.

At the second and third levels the focus is on the school community and the home, with particular attention given to parents. It is parents who have expectations for the school that are often more specific and less objective than those of the wider community. Parents also have a greater and more direct effect upon the input of each individual child into the instructional program. Taken collectively, and because of their intense interest in the school's means and projected ends, the parents generally make up the most influential school-related group and may have the greatest impact upon community awareness and potential educational efforts and political actions within the larger community.

Because of the allocation of tasks and expertise within MUS-E and because of the systematic approach of IGE, parents should be presented with a clear picture of the school's aims regarding the cognitive, affective, and psychomotor development of their children and the procedures used in stimulating such development. This responsibility belongs to the IGE unit staff and is met through the home-school-community relations program. From the point of view of the I & R unit, the reality of the intense family influence on children elucidates the necessity of parental inputs. Not only must the unit teachers understand the home in order to understand the child; they are dependent upon the parents to accept, and preferably to commit themselves to, their instructional program for the individual child.

As noted toward the center of Figure 3-4, teachers utilize the IPM to plan and carry out instruction for each individual child. The figure explicates, further, that the child's family and community influence his attitudes, ability, and skills. The teachers' understanding of these influences and their awareness of the available resources in the home and the community provide them with maximum operational

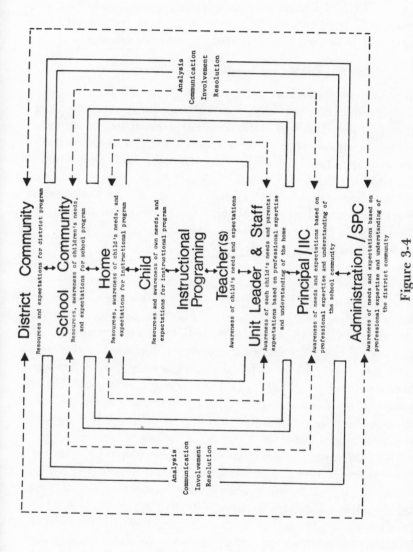

Figure 3-4

Communications and dependencies in a home-school-community relation (from Marvin M. Fruth and Dean Bowles, *A Program of Home-School-Community Relations*, Working Paper [Madison, Wis.: Wisconsin Research and Development Center for Cognitive Learning, in press])

District Community
Resources and expectations for district program

School Community
Resources, awareness of children's needs, and expectations for school program

Home
Resources, awareness of child's needs, and expectations for instructional program

Child
Resources and awareness of own needs, and expectations for instructional program

Instructional Programing

Teacher(s)
Awareness of child's needs and expectations

Unit Leader & Staff
Awareness of each child's needs and parents' expectations based on professional expertise and understanding of the home

Principal /IIC
Awareness of needs and expectations based on professional expertise and understanding of the school community

Administration /SPC
Awareness of needs and expectations based on professional expertise and understanding of the district community

Analysis
Communication
Involvement
Resolution

Analysis
Communication
Involvement
Resolution

output. It is noted that the first materials for use in an in-service program dealing with home-school-community relations were yet under refinement by Fruth and Bowles at the Wisconsin R & D Center as of 1973. Other materials, including a handbook for principals and audiovisual materials for use by teachers and community personnel, were in various stages of planning and development.

Environments that Facilitate IGE Practices

Facilitative environments in school buildings, school district offices, state education agencies, and teacher education institutions are required to maintain and strengthen IGE schools so that, in fact, each school becomes increasingly self-renewing.[16] The three main elements of a facilitative educational environment are: people who are committed to IGE and who have the knowledge and competence to carry out their respective roles; the necessary material resources, including buildings and equipment; and the organizational arrangements that provide the means for human and material resources to be mobilized effectively within the locality, state, and nation.

We saw earlier that the MUS was conceptualized to produce the facilitative environment at the school district level. To provide the facilitative environments nationally, new organizational arrangements may be needed in each of the states. For this purpose a trilevel hierarchy of interlocking groups patterned after the organizational arrangements of the MUS was conceptualized. Included in the hierarchy are members of the state education agency (SEA), teacher education institutions (TEI), and local school districts.[17] Other groups such as teachers' associations and parents' organizations also may share in the policy development and implementation at each of the various organizational levels.

The trilevel hierarchical arrangements that are compatible with the organizational objectives of the MUS are shown in Figure 3-5. At the lowest level is the SPC, which was discussed earlier as the highest point of the MUS organizational-administrative structure. It may be recalled that each SPC includes the administrative officer of the school district or his designee, other members of the central office staff, representative building principals of IGE schools of the district, and representative teachers and unit leaders of the IGE schools of the district.

At the second level of organization is the Regional IGE

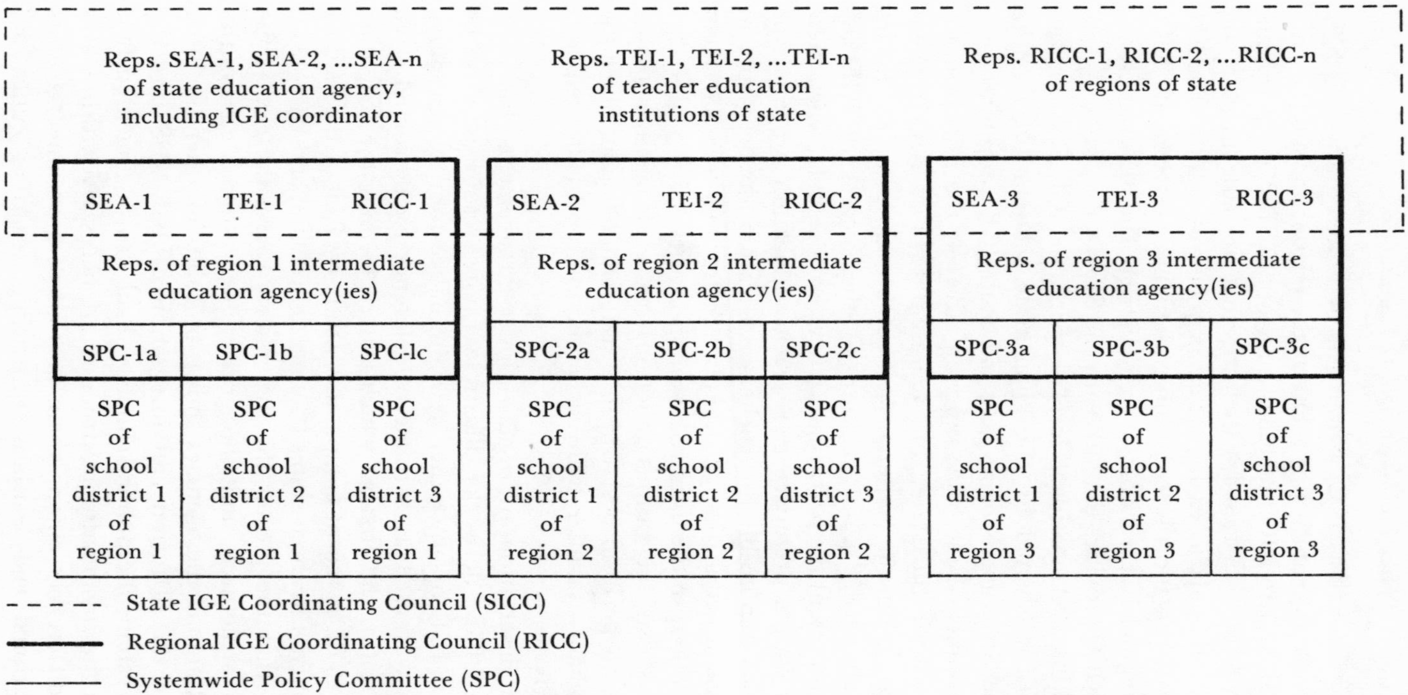

SEA-1, SEA-2, ...SEA-n of state education agency, including IGE coordinator:
Reps. SEA-1, SEA-2, ...SEA-n of state education agency, including IGE coordinator

Reps. TEI-1, TEI-2, ...TEI-n of teacher education institutions of state

Reps. RICC-1, RICC-2, ...RICC-n of regions of state

SEA-1	TEI-1	RICC-1
Reps. of region 1 intermediate education agency(ies)		
SPC-1a	SPC-1b	SPC-1c
SPC of school district 1 of region 1	SPC of school district 2 of region 1	SPC of school district 3 of region 1

SEA-2	TEI-2	RICC-2
Reps. of region 2 intermediate education agency(ies)		
SPC-2a	SPC-2b	SPC-2c
SPC of school district 1 of region 2	SPC of school district 2 of region 2	SPC of school district 3 of region 2

SEA-3	TEI-3	RICC-3
Reps. of region 3 intermediate education agency(ies)		
SPC-3a	SPC-3b	SPC-3c
SPC of school district 1 of region 3	SPC of school district 2 of region 3	SPC of school district 3 of region 3

- - - - State IGE Coordinating Council (SICC)

——— Regional IGE Coordinating Council (RICC)

——— Systemwide Policy Committee (SPC)

Figure 3-5

Prototypic organizational arrangements of a state-regional-local IGE network (from Herbert J. Klausmeier, James E. Walter, and L. Joseph Lins, *Manual for Starting and Maintaining State IGE Networks* [Madison, Wis.: University of Wisconsin/Sears Roebuck Foundation IGE Teacher Education Project, 1974])

Coordinating Council (RICC) comprised of representatives of SPCs of a region, a representative of a TEI of the region, and a representative of the SEA. The RICC includes a regional IGE coordinator and representatives of the agencies that together are able to start and maintain IGE schools in each particular region of a state. The SPC representatives provide the communication link between the RICC and the individual IGE schools of each district. The SEA representative on the RICC provides the link with the SEA.

At the third organizational level is the State IGE Coordinating Council (SICC). Chaired by the chief state school officer or his designee, the SICC includes at least one state IGE coordinator and also key personnel of the SEA, representatives of the TEIs from the various regions of the state, and representatives of RICCs of the regions. Two important criteria for membership here are having specialized knowledge to contribute to the success of IGE and authority to represent the particular agency. For example, when there are plans to start a preservice IGE teacher-education program, the various persons responsible for teacher certification, the development of an IGE teacher-education program in a college, and the placement of student teachers in the local IGE schools are needed.

Table 3-2 shows the various functions that each member agency may be able to perform best within a state and a region. Since the reader is probably familiar with each function, no further explanation will be given.

This brief description of organizational arrangements for state-regional-local IGE networks illustrates how resources may be mobilized for IGE or any other new alternative form of schooling. The pattern was used as a frame of reference by personnel from twenty-one states, the first of which started forming the IGE state networks in 1972. A recent comparative study by Paul of the facilitative environments in three states (Connecticut, Ohio, and Wisconsin) has revealed that the greater the dynamic linkages, the clearer the coordinating structures, and the greater the resource capabilities between and among the agencies shown in Table 3-2, then the more complete are the diffusion and integration of IGE-MUS into the target user system, the public schools.[18] Paul also documented that variations in the organizational structure are necessary within states because of differences among them in kind of governmental units and constitutional and legislative provisions regarding education, area, population, and other characteristics.

Table 3-2

Major functions of the state education agency or regional education agency, teacher education institutions, and local education agencies in implementing IGE

| | | | *Functions* | |
| | Awareness: 1-day conferences | First-year implementation: 3-day PUL workshop, 3-5 day workshop for IGE building staff, in-service during first year of implementation | Maintenance and refinement: short intensive noncredit and credit courses, graduate courses at school sites and on college campus | Institutionalization: preservice IGE teacher education program, graduate program for IGE unit leaders and staff teachers, graduate program for IGE building principals and other administrators |
Responsible agency				
State education agency or regional agencies of SEA	1[a]	1	2	2
Teacher education institution	2	3	1	1
Local education agency	3 (for its own schools)	2 (for its own schools)	3 (for its own schools)	

[a] 1 indicates that the agency will probably take major initiative in most states; 2 indicates that the agency is less likely to take major initiative, but should be involved in planning; and 3 indicates least likelihood for assuming primary responsibility for the function.

Source: Klausmeier, Walter, and Lins, *Manual for Starting and Maintaining State IGE Networks.*

Continuing Research and Development to Improve IGE

The seventh and final component of IGE is continuing development and development-based research to produce validated instructional materials and procedures. In addition, other research to generate knowledge and theory dealing with instruction, learning, and the various components of IGE is necessary since IGE is a dynamic system that must change and continuously improve. The various kinds of research and development related to IGE may be illustrated briefly.

Local schools continuously conduct evaluative research when implementing the IPM and evaluating its effectiveness. Larger school districts and state education agencies also evaluate their IGE programs. Development and development-based research are carried out by the Wisconsin R & D Center to develop each component of IGE already discussed, including curriculum materials and measurement tools. The development of the specific IGE components and also of other comprehensive educational products requires specialized capabilities such as are found in research and development centers, regional educational laboratories, state education agencies, and profit and nonprofit corporations, as described in Klausmeier and O'Hearn.[19]

Long-term development and refinement of curriculum materials and procedures related to reading, mathematics, motivation, and the like require cooperative efforts of many individuals and agencies. Subject-matter specialists, methodologists, and behavioral scientists provide the essential input of substantive and procedural knowledge. School personnel and those from the state education agency assist in determining how well the new materials and methods work. Through an interactive cycle of developing the materials, testing them in school settings, and revising as necessary, the Wisconsin R & D Center produces materials for particular target groups of children, teachers, and other educational personnel. In the final cycle, information is secured to determine how well the children learn from the material or procedure in its almost final form, how much time is required on the part of the teacher to use it, and how well the teachers like it.

Knowledge-generating research has many variants including short-term horizontal descriptive research and controlled experimentation.[20] Usually this research is not directly related to the instructional program of the school, although it could be, and the results often have neither immediate nor long-term implications for improving IGE or any other form of schooling. Despite this, the research may be highly significant in extending knowledge about a component of the instructional system or refining theory related to children's learning and development.

In 1965 the staff of local school districts independently, of the Wisconsin R & D Center independently, or of both agencies cooperatively began to engage in the preceding activities; the related technical reports of the activities are listed in annual annotated bibliographies of the publications of the Wisconsin R & D Center.

The major continuing research thrusts of the Wisconsin R & D Center as of 1974, in addition to the development and evaluation of products, deal with children's learning and development; the IPM and related computer management of IGE instruction; organizational roles, staffing, and staff relationships in IGE schools; cost-effectiveness of IGE schooling; and the extension of IGE to the middle and high school levels.[21]

Origin and Diffusion of IGE

Continuing cooperative efforts by many persons and agencies have been required to develop the various components of IGE, start the early IGE schools, and carry out the implementation process in many school districts and many states. Different from a curriculum package that can be distributed commercially and then used by teachers without in-service education, IGE requires many changes within schools that are possible only as there is early in-service education, followed by continuing staff development within each IGE school. Added difficulties were encountered in implementing IGE because the U.S. Office of Education, until about 1971, did not formulate an implementation plan and provide funding for the products whose development it supported. It may be instructive, therefore, to consider a few milestones in the development and implementation of IGE.

IGE started in embryonic form when a project called Maximizing Opportunities for Development and Experimentation in Learning in the Schools (MODELS) was begun at the Wisconsin R & D Center under the direction of the present author as principal investigator.[22]

As a first practical result of this project, four school districts, with the assistance of personnel from the R & D Center, started the first thirteen nongraded I & R units as replacements for age-graded classes in schools of Madison, Janesville, Milwaukee, and Racine, Wisconsin, in the second semester of the school year 1965-1966.[23]

In 1966-1967 the number of functioning I & R units increased to nineteen. The following year seven elementary schools for the first time completely organized into I & R units, and the term "multiunit" elementary school (MUS-E) was coined to designate these schools.[24] Also, the other two elements of the organizational-administrative arrangements, the IIC of each school building and the SPC, were started.

The Wisconsin Department of Public Instruction (DPI) selected the MUS-E for statewide demonstration and implementation during the school year 1968-1969. Thereafter, as IGE implementers were educated regarding IGE, as materials and programs were developed to assist local schools in changing to IGE, and as many agencies became involved in implementation, the number of IGE/MUS-Es increased rapidly with totals as follows: 50 in 1969-1970, 500 in 1971-1972, and between 1,500 and 2,000 in 1973-1974. Projections for the future indicate that accelerated expansion will continue throughout the 1970s. Some events associated with the rapid and continuing growth merit brief attention.

In 1968 the R & D Center, with consultation from personnel of the Wisconsin DPI and local schools, developed a book and fifteen videotapes for use in implementation by the DPI, the R & D Center, and other interested educational agencies. These materials were used until 1971. In 1969 the R & D Center and the Institute for Development of Educational Activities (/I/D/E/A/) signed an agreement whereby /I/D/E/A/ was authorized to use the preceding materials in producing a more sophisticated set. /I/D/E/A/ incorporated into the new materials insights from its own study of educational change. Beginning in 1970-1971 /I/D/E/A/ used these IGE "Change Program" materials to prepare "facilitators" to start MUS-Es.[25]

The R & D Center also used the same materials until 1972 when the /I/D/E/A/ implementation strategy and conditions for use of the materials were judged incompatible with the strategy of the R & D Center. The R & D Center then developed new MUS-E in-service materials and combined them with other in-service materials dealing with its several IGE curriculum and instructional components.

Early in 1971 the MUS-E was selected by the U.S. Office of Education for nationwide implementation, and this brought the R & D Center into its first wide-scale implementation effort. The R & D Center was funded by three federal agencies to carry out certain parts of a comprehensive implementation strategy during 1971-1972 and 1972-1973. The National Institute of Education funded a small effort during 1973-1974. In preparation for the national effort, a four-phase implementation strategy was formulated; it consisted of awareness, first-year implementation, second-year maintenance and refinement and institutionalization.[26]

The R & D Center carried out the awareness phase only once in 1971. First-year implementation was coordinated primarily by coordinators of nine state education agencies: Colorado, Connecticut, Illinois, Indiana, Minnesota, New Jersey, Ohio, South Carolina, and Wisconsin—and by other agencies in California, Nebraska, New York, and Virginia. The R & D Center did not receive sufficient funding to respond to the interest in the other states. Approximately 275 IGE schools were started each year in these states. Maintenance and refinement activities, in the form of one-week institutes for experienced IGE personnel, were conducted by seven teacher education institutions of Wisconsin, Ohio, and Connecticut. Approximately 700 unit leaders, 300 building principals, and 100 reading staff teachers of functioning IGE schools attended these institutes.[27] Institutionalization (defined as teacher education institutions developing on-campus programs and preparing building principals and unit leaders for their IGE roles) was started in 1971-1972 with federal support. The support was provided only for that year.

In 1972 the Sears-Roebuck Foundation invited a proposal that led to funding of the UW/IGE Teacher Education Project.[28] The major activity of the UW/SRF IGE Teacher Education Project is to develop printed and audiovisual instructional materials for use in undergraduate programs to prepare teachers for IGE schools and in graduate programs to prepare staff teachers, unit leaders, building principals, and other administrators for IGE service. The second activity of this project is to assist personnel of sixteen states to form state IGE networks, coordinated by the respective state education agencies. The mutual expectations are that the education agencies and teacher education institutions of each state will have the capability to start and maintain IGE schools, to prepare prospective IGE teachers through on-campus programs, and to prepare unit leaders and building principals for service in IGE schools through on-campus graduate programs.

Another significant event is that the IGE coordinators of twelve states took the initiative in establishing a national IGE organization in 1973: the Association for Individually Guided Education.

Formative Evaluation of IGE Components

The R & D Center and other agencies have not been funded at a sufficient level to carry out desired comprehensive and systematic evaluations of IGE annually. Despite this limitation, many formative evaluations of the organization-administrative arrangements have been completed and are reported briefly. Evaluative studies dealing with other components are discussed at the end of the chapter.

Attaining Process Objectives during First-Year Changeover

The Educational Testing Service (ETS) of Princeton, New Jersey, was contracted by the U.S. Office of Education to evaluate the effectiveness of the changeover to IGE made by some 275 schools during the school year 1971-1972.[29] Ironside of ETS conducted the evaluation.

The R & D Center and the cooperating state education agency specified the four minimum accomplishments to be attained by each IGE school by the end of its first year: the entire school should be organized into I & R units with each unit attaining outcomes specified for the unit; there should be multiage grouping of children in the units; each I & R unit should carry out instruction in at least one curriculum area according to the model of instructional programming for the individual student; and there should be a functioning IIC that included the principal and the unit leaders and that attained outcomes as specified by the R & D Center for the IIC. The principal conclusion drawn by Ironside was: "All evidences point toward the conclusion that the MUS-E/IGE organizational and instructional changes have *taken hold* in the majority of schools responding to the follow-up. Apparently attrition has been slight if existent at all, and many schools have come closer to institutionalizing the two areas of innovation [MUS-organizational arrangement and instructional programing model]."[30]

Ironside made several useful suggestions to current and potential IGE implementers in state education agencies, teacher education institutions, and local school districts, one of them being "the follow-up study verifies the admonition that MUS-E/IGE implementation may take 3 or 4 years (in terms of local satisfaction and in terms of fulfilling the many implementation criteria). Some school people, researchers, and coordinators have perhaps hoped that the major hurdles could be mastered in the first year by most schools; this appears a questionable assumption at best, in view of the data reported here."[31]

Cost of Changeover

Evers collected data on a random sample of thirty-nine schools in eight states, stratified according to three sizes of enrollment, to ascertain the cost of changing over to IGE during the first year, 1971-1972.[32] The main results were that the majority of schools did not increase or decrease the number of instructional and noninstructional staff, except paid paraprofessionals; had an increase in the cost of staff development, the median being $500 per school, and an increase in cost for in-service materials, the median being $250 per school; had no increase or decrease in costs related to pupil absenteeism, pupil vandalism, salaries of instructional personnel, consultant services, instructional materials and equipment, and school plant and furnishing; and used their instructional materials and equipment more effectively than before the changeover to IGE.

The above results are in line with earlier suggestions from the R & D Center regarding additional costs during the first two years of changeover. The first suggestion was to allocate at least ten dollars per pupil during the first two years for any combination of one instructional aide per 150 children, additional instructional materials, and higher pay for the unit leader. The second concerned remodeling the "egg-crate" type of school building so that there would be one well-supplied instructional resource center to accommodate at least ninety intermediate-age children and another center to accommodate at least sixty primary-age children. The third suggestion regarded participation in a staff development program starting with a one-day workshop for chief school officers, a three-day workshop for the prospective building principal and unit leaders of the various MUS-Es, a one-week workshop for the entire staff of each MUS-E prior to the opening of the MUS-E in the fall (this could be spread out during a semester), four half-day workshops for the entire staff of each building during the first year, and a one-week institute for central office consultants in the curriculum area that would be given most attention during the first year. In Wisconsin the Department of Public Instruction and local school districts have been implementing this program since 1968.[33]

Attaining Organizational Objectives

Pellegrin of the Center for Advanced Study of Education Administration (CASEA) in 1968 studied an IGE and a control school in each of three Wisconsin school systems that were completing their first year in the IGE pattern.[34] His main conclusions were that various kinds of specialization of work by the instructional staff of I & R units were emerging in the IGE schools; cooperative working relationships and open communication among the instructional staff and the principal were higher in the IGE schools; shared decision making about instruction and other matters was occurring in the I & R units; commitment had been made by the staff of the IGE schools to the objective of providing for differences among students in rate and style of learning; and teacher morale was higher in IGE schools.

Recognizing that Pellegrin's findings were based upon only the first three IGE schools of the nation in their first year of functioning, Herrick examined and compared organizational structures and teacher motivation in thirty-four IGE/MUS-E and thirty-eight non-IGE/MUS-E schools.[35] He discovered that IGE schools were significantly less centralized in their decision-making structure and significantly less stratified in terms of status differences among staff than were non-IGE schools. Also the teachers in IGE schools were clearly more highly motivated to do their jobs than were teachers in non-IGE schools, especially when rewards for teaching performance were related to social relations, fringe benefits, and opportunities for meaningful participation in educational planning.

Smith reported a study of thirty-one elementary schools that had changed over to the multiunit organizational pattern in September 1970.[36] Two interesting conclusions about matters associated with the functioning of IICs were that the compatibility of IIC members was strongly related to the effectiveness of the IIC and that the amount of administrative experience of principals was not connected with the effectiveness of the IIC, but the amount of consideration shown by the principal to other staff members was highly related to his degree of experience.

Walter examined the relationship between organizational structure and adaptiveness in twenty IGE/MUS-E and eighteen non-IGE/ MUS-E schools and reported that IGE schools were significantly lower in centralization of decision making and were significantly higher in adaptiveness.[37]

Without exception the foregoing studies show that IGE schools rate significantly higher than the non-IGE schools on a host of organizational variables—involvement in decision making, shared responsibilities, work specialization, power distribution, and shared status—all of which characterize the dynamic, as opposed to the mechanistic, organization. To move beyond comparative studies of IGE and non-IGE schools, Lipham has proposed that longitudinal studies be conducted that focus upon changes in decision roles, decision content, decision involvement, and leadership styles as schools move into IGE/MUS-E.[38]

Attaining Objectives in the Cognitive Domain

Among the performance criteria set for IGE schools by the R & D Center and various state education agencies, one calls for the school to implement programming for the individual student in at least one curriculum area by the end of the first year of operation.[39] A curriculum area incorporating the IPM is the WDRSD. The WDRSD includes a Word Attack element in which subskills have been identified, the mastery of which are presumed to lead to independence in attacking phonetically and structurally regular words.[40] The Word Attack tests were administered in two IGE schools to groups of pupils beginning their second, third, and fourth years of schooling in September 1969, when the WDRSD was introduced, and again one year later in September 1970 to the same groups who then were beginning their third, fourth, and fifth years, respectively. In addition to identifying the gains made by each group, the achievements of three groups who had not experienced the WDRSD program by the fall of 1969 were compared with three groups who had experienced the program for one year by the fall of 1970. A higher percent of those who had participated in the program, in comparison with the baseline children, achieved mastery of twenty-three skills, fewer mastered six skills, and an equal percent mastered one skill.

A published norm-referenced test, the Doren Diagnostic Reading Test, was administered to the baseline and experienced groups of children toward the end of their third year of schooling in May 1969 and again in May 1970. In both schools the means for the WDRSD groups were higher.[41] The higher reading achievement was attributed to the combined effects of multiunit organization and a concerted attack on curriculum improvement in reading in accordance with programming for the individual student.

Attaining Objectives in the Affective Domain

Nelson, using self-report inventories, compared the responses of pupils from thirteen IGE schools and twelve traditional elementary schools of the same districts (one district could not supply a comparable control school).[42] His main conclusions were that the self-concepts of the pupils in the IGE schools were higher than in the traditional schools, the pupils' attitudes toward fellow pupils in IGE schools were higher than in traditional schools, and the two groups were about the same in their attitudes toward teachers and instruction and in school morale.

Directions for IGE in the 1970s

Questions may be raised in the national context as to whether IGE will become available to large numbers of school personnel and children as an alternative to the traditional age-graded system of elementary education and also to departmentalized elementary schooling. There are two main requirements for a larger number of more effective IGE schools.

First, instructional programming for the individual student is readily understood by teachers and is functioning well in some schools in some curriculum areas. Some teachers, however, do not receive the essential in-service education to understand it. Also, there remains a shortage of curriculum materials compatible with related criterion-referenced assessment tools in most curriculum areas. The available compatible materials are relatively expensive in comparison with traditional instructional materials. Many regular materials used in a good number of IGE schools presume a strong reliance on a verbal type of instruction and therefore are not effective with children who are low in verbal abilities. It would be helpful in implementing the IPM to have less time-consuming and less expensive means for the frequent assessment of children's achievements, recording of their accomplishments, and identifying of appropriate alternative instructional sequences. Economically feasible computer-managed instruction is clearly needed, but is not yet available.

Second, a substantial number of schools have made the initial changeover to IGE successfully—about 1,500 to 2,000 of the 75,000 elementary schools in the U.S. as of 1973-1974. A greater cooperative effort involving state education agencies, teacher education institutions, and local school districts in the in-service education of the school staffs of entire buildings is, however, needed to optimize the effectiveness of these schools. Also, more cooperation is necessary for the same agencies to prepare school personnel to perform in IGE as well as in other kinds of schools. Until substantial numbers of unit leaders, principals, and teachers are prepared adequately for their roles in IGE schools, those schools desiring to make the changeover will be unable to do so. Materials and strategies already developed for in-service education, projected materials under development for use in on-campus programs, and provisions for educating leadership personnel from all three agencies appear to be adequate to provide the necessary information base for both the in-service and on-campus programs.[43]

Appendix. List of IGE Acronyms

IGE Organizational and Instructional Acronyms

I & R	Instructional and Research Unit (classroom level)
IGE	Individually Guided Education
IIC	Instructional Improvement Committee (school building level)
IPM	Instructional Programming Model
MUS	Multiunit School Organization
MUS-E	Multiunit School Organization-Elementary
RICC	Regional IGE Coordinating Council
SICC	State IGE Coordinating Council
SPC	Systemwide Policy Committee (school district level)

IGE Curriculum Acronyms

DMP   Developing Mathematical Processes

IGM   Individually Guided Motivation

WDRSD   Wisconsin Design for Reading Skill Development

Notes

1. Education USA, Special Report, *Individually Guided Education and the Multiunit School* (Arlington, Va.: National School Public Relations Association 1972).

2. Herbert J. Klausmeier, *Individually Guided Education: An Alternative System of Elementary Schooling*, delivered as the Harland E. Anderson Lecture at Yale University (New Haven, Conn.: Institute for Social and Policy Studies, Yale University, 1972). I should like to acknowledge the continuing support of the Wisconsin Research and Development Center for Cognitive Learning in the initial conceptualization and later description of IGE in its totality as an alternative form of schooling. Persons who worked closely with me in these activities are recognized in citations as joint authors.

3. A more complete description of the components and the related in-service education requirements for making the initial changeover to IGE are given in Herbert J. Klausmeier, Mary R. Quilling, Juanita S. Sorenson, Russell S. Way, and George R. Glasrud, *Individually Guided Education and the Multiunit Elementary School: Guidelines for Implementation* (Madison, Wis.: Wisconsin Research and Development Center for Cognitive Learning, 1971).

4. Herbert J. Klausmeier and Roland J. Pellegrin, "The Multiunit School: A Differentiated Staffing Approach," in *Planned Change in Education*, ed. D. S. Bushnell and D. Rappaport (New York: Harcourt, Brace, Jovanovich, 1971), 107-26.

5. Terrance J. Sheridan, "Perceived Role and Effectiveness of the Unit Leader in Conducting Unit Functions," unpublished doctoral dissertation, University of Wisconsin, Madison, 1974.

6. Herbert J. Klausmeier, Juanita S. Sorenson, and Mary R. Quilling, "Instructional Programming for the Individual Pupil in the Multiunit Elementary School," *Elementary School Journal* 72 (November 1971): 88-101.

7. Wayne Otto and Eunice N. Askov, *Wisconsin Design for Reading Skill Development: Rationale and Guidelines* (Minneapolis, Minn.: National Computer Systems, 1973).

8. Herbert J. Klausmeier, Jan T. Jeter, Mary R. Quilling, and Dorothy A. Frayer, *Individually Guided Motivation* (Madison, Wis.: Wisconsin Research and Development Center for Cognitive Learning, 1973).

9. C. Mauritz Lindvall and John O. Belvin, "Programed Instruction in the Schools: An Application of Programing Principles in 'Individually Prescribed Instruction,' " in *Programed Instruction*, ed. Phil C. Lange, Sixty-sixth Yearbook of the National Society for the Study of Education, Part II (Chicago: University of Chicago Press, 1967), 217-54.

10. Sidney L. Belt and Denis W. Spuck, *Computer Applications in Individually Guided Education: A Computer-Based System for Instructional Management (WIS-SIM): Needs and Specifications* (Madison, Wis.: Wisconsin Research and Development Center for Cognitive Learning, 1973).

11. Herbert J. Klausmeier and William L. Goodwin, *Learning and Human Abilities: Educational Psychology*, 4th ed. (New York: Harper and Row, in press).

12. John C. Flanagan, "Project PLAN," paper given at the Aerospace Education Foundation Seminar on Education for the 1970s, Washington, D. C. (Palo Alto, Calif.: American Institutes for Research, 1967).

13. Klausmeier *et al.*, *Individually Guided Education*.

14. *IGE News* (Madison, Wis.: Wisconsin Research and Development Center for Cognitive Learning, Fall 1973).

15. Marvin M. Fruth and Dean Bowles, "A Program of Home-School-Community Relations," Working Paper (Madison, Wis.: Wisconsin Research and Development Center for Cognitive Learning, in press).

16. Klausmeier *et al.*, *Individually Guided Education*.

17. Herbert J. Klausmeier, James E. Walter, and L. Joseph Lins, *Manual for Starting and Maintaining State IGE Networks* (Madison, Wis.: University of Wisconsin/Sears-Roebuck Foundation IGE Teacher Education Project, 1974).

18. Douglas A. Paul, "The Diffusion of an Innovation through Inter-organization Linkages," unpublished doctoral dissertation, University of Wisconsin, Madison, 1974.

19. *Research and Development toward the Improvement of Education*, ed. Herbert J. Klausmeier and George T. O'Hearn (Madison, Wis.: Dembar Educational Research Services, 1968).

20. Lee J. Cronbach and Patrick Suppes, *Research for Tomorrow's Schools: Disciplined Inquiry for Education* (New York: Macmillan, 1969).

21. Richard R. Rossmiller, "Individually Guided Education," in *Handbook on Contemporary Education*, ed. S. E. Goodman (New York: Xerox Corporation through R. R. Bowker Company, in press).

22. Herbert J. Klausmeier, William L. Goodwin, John Prasch, and Max R. Goodson, with an introduction by Warren G. Findley, *Project MODELS: Maximizing Opportunities for Development and Experimentation in Learning in the Schools*, Occasional Paper No. 3 (Madison, Wis.: Wisconsin Research and Development Center for Cognitive Learning, 1966).

23. Herbert J. Klausmeier, Doris M. Cook, William L. Goodwin, Glenn E. Tagatz, and Louis Pingel, *Individualizing Instruction in Language Arts through Development and Research in R & I Units of Local Schools, 1965-1966*, Technical Report No. 19 (Madison, Wis.: Wisconsin Research and Development Center for Cognitive Learning, 1967).

24. Klausmeier and O'Hearn, *Research and Development toward the Improvement of Education*.

25. Education USA, Special Report, *op. cit.*

26. Herbert J. Klausmeier, *Project Plan and Budget Request for the Nationwide Installation of Multiunit Schools* (Madison, Wis.: Wisconsin Research and

Development Center for Cognitive Learning, 1971). The author acknowledges the assistance of Lee Burchinal, then of the U.S. Office of Education, and Professor Thomas Romberg in the initial formulation of a four-phase implementation strategy. Many persons of the R & D Center and of state and local education agencies and teacher education institutions have contributed to its refinement and practice.

27. William Sipes, *Preliminary Report on Results of One-Week Institutes for Experienced Multiunit Personnel* (Madison, Wis.: Wisconsin Research and Development Center for Cognitive Learning, 1972).

28. Herbert J. Klausmeier, *An Invitation to the Sears-Roebuck Foundation to Improve Elementary Schooling through Implementation, Refinement, and Institutionalization of IGE/MUS-E* (Madison, Wis.: School of Education, University of Wisconsin, 1972).

29. Roderick A. Ironside, *The 1971-72 Nationwide Installation of the Multiunit/IGE Model for Elementary Schools: A Process Evaluation* (Princeton, N.J.: Educational Testing Service, 1973).

30. Roderick A. Ironside, *A Supplement to the 1971-72 Nationwide Installation of the Multiunit/IGE Model for Elementary Schools: A Process Evaluation* (Princeton, N.J.: Educational Testing Service, 1973), 5.

31. *Ibid.*, 39.

32. Nancy A. Evers, *IGE/MUS-E First Year Implementation Cost Survey*, Technical Report No. 256 (Madison, Wis.: Wisconsin Research and Development Center for Cognitive Learning, 1973).

33. Herbert J. Klausmeier, "The Multiunit Elementary School and Individually Guided Education," *Phi Delta Kappan* 53 (November 1971): 181-84.

34. Roland J. Pellegrin, Allen T. Slagle, and Lloyd Johansen, "Some Organizational Characteristics of Multiunit Schools," mimeographed working paper no. 22 (Madison, Wis.: Wisconsin Research and Development Center for Cognitive Learning, 1969).

35. H. Scott Herrick, "Organizational Structure and Teacher Motivation in Multiunit and Nonmultiunit Schools," unpublished doctoral dissertation, University of Wisconsin, Madison, 1974.

36. Kenneth B. Smith, *An Analysis of the Relationship between Effectiveness of the Multiunit Elementary School's Instructional Improvement Committee and Interpersonal and Leader Behaviors*, Technical Report No. 230 (Madison, Wis.: Wisconsin Research and Development Center for Cognitive Learning, 1972).

37. James E. Walter, "The Relationship of Organizational Structure to Organizational Adaptiveness in Elementary Schools," unpublished doctoral dissertation, University of Wisconsin, Madison, 1973.

38. James M. Lipham, *Individual-Organizational Articulation in IGE Schools* (Madison, Wis.: Wisconsin Research and Development Center for Cognitive Learning, in press).

39. Herbert J. Klausmeier, Mary R. Quilling, and Juanita S. Sorenson, *The Development and Evaluation of the Multiunit Elementary School, 1966-1970*, Technical Report No. 158 (Madison, Wis.: Wisconsin Research and Development Center for Cognitive Learning, 1971).

40. Otto and Askov, *op. cit.*

41. Klausmeier *et al.*, *Development and Evaluation of the Multiunit Elementary School.*

42. R. G. Nelson, *An Analysis of the Relationship of the Multiunit Elementary School Organizational Structure and Individually Guided Education to the Learning Climate of Pupils*, Technical Report No. 213 (Madison, Wis.: Wisconsin Research and Development Center for Cognitive Learning, 1972).

43. Formative evaluation reports on the Curriculum and Instructional components of IGE, published by the Wisconsin Research and Development Center for Cognitive Learning, may be obtained by writing Professor Herbert J. Klausmeier, Wisconsin Research and Development Center for Cognitive Learning, 1025 W. Johnson Street, Madison, Wisconsin 53706.

4. Adaptive Environments for Learning: Curriculum Aspects

Robert Glaser and *Jerome Rosner*

The central concern of the Learning Research and Development Center (LRDC) since its inception has been the investigation of ways in which elementary schools can be more adaptive to individual differences than generally has been possible in school settings. From

The Learning Research and Development Center is a university-based institute funded primarily at its outset by the Office of Education, United States Department of Health, Education, and Welfare. Presently the center is supported in part by the National Institute of Education, United States Department of Health, Education, and Welfare. For the work described in this chapter, additional support was received from the Ford Foundation, the National Science Foundation, General Learning Corporation, Appleton-Century-Crofts, Imperial International Learning Corporation, and Walker Educational Book Corporation. The authors' opinions do not necessarily reflect the position or policy of the sponsoring agencies, and no official endorsement should be inferred. The work of LRDC is the work of many individuals: the research associates and their staffs at the center, educational researchers in the field, teachers and school administrators, university graduate students and elementary school children, and encouraging parents and school boards. We have chosen to describe here the work of LRDC by quoting from published material of the curriculum developers. The limitations of space made major abridgments necessary, but all excerpts are carefully referenced so that the reader can explore a particular topic more thoroughly.

the beginning, our enterprise has been one of constant interrogation of the operational requirements for adaptive educational environments. A first step was taken in 1964 in conjunction with the forward-looking Baldwin-Whitehall (Pennsylvania) School District that had just completed building the Oakleaf Elementary School. We decided, with them, to bypass an extensive planning stage and install an individualized progress system throughout Oakleaf, a kindergarten through grade six school, with an enrollment of approximately 350 children. Over the course of a preliminary year, curricula were assembled in a number of school subjects from a variety of existing materials.

LRDC and Oakleaf sought a program of continuing practical experience so that the processes involved could be observed and studied to determine what further requirements evolved. It soon became apparent that curriculum materials then available were not completely satisfactory for individualized instruction. These materials were designed for conventional classroom teaching; they were not based on the hierarchical analysis of subject matter required for both the effective diagnosis of student prerequisites and the alternative paths required for individual student progress. For this reason LRDC became involved in curriculum development in elementary mathematics, reading, science, and the preschool-kindergarten skills that seemed necessary to ensure the readiness required for continued successful school achievement. The individually prescribed instruction procedure in mathematics was completed first and came to be known as IPI Math.[1]

In 1963, because of the urgency of the urban school problem, LRDC started a second developmental school, the Frick School, in cooperation with the Pittsburgh City Schools. The initial emphasis in the Frick School was the development of preparatory skills at the preschool and kindergarten levels. For this purpose, the Primary Education Program (PEP) was launched as the early learning extension of our concern with the design of adaptive educational environments. In this program, with a longer lead time than was possible in our initial efforts, curriculum learning hierarchies were analyzed in more depth than had been done in the past.

It became increasingly apparent that a school environment is a complex organization of two broadly defined interacting domains: classroom environmental conditions, such as motivational factors, social climate, and the organization of classroom time and space; and instructional program conditions, such as the nature of the curricula in use and the way the teachers use them. This chapter will focus exclusively on one aspect of the latter domain—the nature of curricular components in a school that is adaptive to individual differences. We will not attempt to address such aspects as the design of the school day, the management of individual progress by the teacher or through student self-management, and studies of classroom motivation practices. Neither will we discuss the issues fundamental to educational development that arise in instructional psychology and evaluation research.[2]

In describing the curricular components designed for an adaptive elementary school environment it is important to make clear two underlying premises of adaptive education: first, children display a wide range of differences in the ways in which they learn and acquire competence; second, children display a wide range of differences in their entering abilities and talents—the skills, aptitudes, and information they bring with them to the first-grade classroom. An adaptive school environment not only attempts to match a child's abilities to alternate ways of learning, but also tries to bring a child's abilities into a range of competence that enhances his potential to profit from the instructional alternatives available in that school.

Thus, given these two premises, one can see that it is the responsibility of elementary education to provide instructional situations (for example, classroom organization, instructional materials, teacher practices) that accommodate the needs of different students, and, when needed, to teach the readiness abilities called for by the instructional situations available. Acceptance of these responsibilities by the school signals a shift from a selective mode of education where the outcomes of education are maximized only for children with the abilities to profit from the instructional conditions provided to an adaptive mode of education that accommodates a wider range of abilities.[3]

This chapter describes curricular components that meet these two fundamental requirements of adaptive education. Three curricula are described that provide alternate paths for learning: IPI Mathematics, the New Primary Grade Reading System, and Individualized Science. We describe, in addition, two other programs designed to have an impact on children's entering abilities and readiness skills related to subsequent school performance: **PEP** and the Perceptual Skills Curriculum. It will be evident that while all these programs apply the concepts of individualization generally described in the initial IPI work, they elaborate on them in different ways. It will be further apparent that the LRDC model of adaptive education has continued to evolve. Our ideas of how best to design a school environment that adapts to individual differences have changed and are still changing as a function of extensive experience in practical school operation, in the methodology of evaluation, and in the psychology of learning and human development.

Instructional Programs that Accommodate Individual Differences

The structure of the programs designed for adaptive learning environments follow certain general instructional guidelines: the goals of learning are specified in terms of student performance and of the conditions under which this performance is to be manifested; the learner's initial capabilities relevant to forthcoming instruction are assessed; educational alternatives suited to the student's initial capabilities are presented to him, and the student selects or is assigned one of these alternatives; the student's performance is monitored and continuously assessed as he learns; instruction proceeds as a function of the relationship among measures of student performance, available instructional alternatives, and criteria of competence; and, as instruction proceeds, data are generated for monitoring and improving the instructional system.[4]

Beginning Concepts: IPI Mathematics

Building on these principles, a program for individualizing instruction was begun.[5] Inherent in this task was the attempt to answer the following question: What relationships exist between individual capabilities and instructional methods that facilitate learning, achievement, and other expressed goals of effective education? We needed a sustained design of educational environments in which the functional relationships between individual differences and learning method could be examined, and for which appropriate evaluative methodology could be developed. School situations were established in which one could adapt to individual differences and from which two kinds of data could be obtained to analyze measurements of individual difference that are relevant to teaching practices, and to assess the effects of alternate procedures for adapting to individual differences.

Requirements for Individual Progress

It was assumed that, in general, an instructional system adaptive to individual differences would display certain characteristics.

First, the conventional boundaries of grade levels and arbitrary time units for subject-matter coverage would be redesigned to permit each student to work at his actual level of accomplishment in a subject-matter area and to permit him to move ahead as soon as he mastered the prerequisites for the next level of advancement.

Second, well-defined sequences of progressive, behaviorally defined objectives in various subject areas would be established as guidelines for setting up a student's program of study.

Third, a student's progress through a curriculum sequence would be monitored by adequate methods and instruments for assessing his abilities and accomplishments so that a teaching program could be adapted to his requirements.

Fourth, students would be taught and provided with appropriate instructional materials so that they could acquire increasing competence in self-directed learning. To accomplish this the teacher would provide the student with standards of performance so that he could evaluate his own attainment, and teaching activities would be directed by the accomplishments of individual learners.

Fifth, school personnel would be provided with special professional training in order that they might evaluate, diagnose, and guide student performance in an individualized setting, as contrasted with managing the learning of a total class.

Sixth, the individualization of instruction would require that the teacher attend to and utilize detailed information about each student in order to design appropriate instructional programs. To assist the teacher in processing this information, schools would probably take advantage of efficient data-processing systems.

The technical requirements for designing and implementing such a system are demanding. The questions involved in measuring individual differences in learning and performance, in making adequate diagnoses of students, in building appropriate learning materials, and in matching student differences to instructional alternatives—all these are the questions that need to be formulated and answered. We shall discuss here some major aspects of the problem and indicate some of the questions that have been raised in our attempts to individualize an elementary school curriculum.

Definition of Educational Objectives

One of the most important factors that contributes to improvement in educational attainment in an individualized system is the analysis and specification of the desired outcomes of learning. Toward this end, the following points are relevant.

The definition of instructional objectives instructs the curriculum designer and the teacher on how to proceed. But vague specification of the desired competence level does not give the teacher enough concrete information about what to look for in student performance and about what to provide to the student to enable him to attain or surpass this performance.

The interaction between the specification of objectives and experience in teaching frequently provides a basis for a redefinition of objectives. The process of clarifying goals, working toward them, appraising progress, reexamining the objectives, modifying the instructional procedures to achieve goals, and clarifying the objectives themselves in the light of experience and data should be a continuous process.

Regardless of the way a subject matter is structured, some hierarchy of subobjectives exists that indicates that certain performances must be present as a basis for learning subsequent tasks. Absence of the specification of prerequisite competence in a sequence of instruction dooms many students to failure.

A student's knowledge of objectives gives him a goal to attain; such knowledge is instructive and motivating. It permits the student to monitor his partial successes and failures and to adjust and organize learning resources for himself.

As in other lines of endeavor, teachers require frequent information about the results of their work so that they can adjust their practices accordingly. Teachers need standards by which to judge themselves and by which society can judge their effectiveness.

The exercise of specifying objectives makes inadequacies and omissions in a curriculum obvious. The fear of many educators that the detailed specification of objectives limits them to only simple behaviors that can be forced into measurable and observable terms is an incorrect notion. If, indeed, complex reasoning and open-endedness are desirable aspects of human behavior, then this needs to be a recognized and measurable goal. Objectives that are too general may force us to settle for what can be easily expressed and measured.

Assessment and Diagnosis

A second major requirement in an individualized program is assessment and diagnosis of the performance of the student so that the amount and kind of instruction can be adapted to his particular requirements. From this point of view, testing and teaching are inseparable aspects and not two different enterprises, as one might be led to believe by current practices in education. Frequent information about student performance is the basis on which the teacher decides the next instructional step. It also serves as feedback to the student. The information is also invaluable for the design and redesign of teaching materials.

The kind of measurement required for these purposes forces a distinction between measurement of performance and measurement of aptitude. The instruments used to measure performance are specifically concerned with the properties of present behavior as they relate to the requirements for deciding on subsequent instructional steps. It seems easier, in a sense, to predict the next lesson in a sequence than to predict long-range performance, which is a task usually set for measuring aptitude. It is possible that measures predictive of immediate learning success are different from those employed for more long-range prediction. Some of the factor studies of changing ability constellations over learning suggest that this may be the case.[6]

The testing procedure designed under the direction of Richard C. Cox, with the evaluation support of C. M. Lindvall, was oriented toward mastery of subject matter. For every unit in mathematics, there were a pretest and a posttest. A pretest samples the various objectives in the unit and is diagnostic enough to pinpoint mastery or the lack of it in the various component skills. A posttest assesses the material that a student has been taught and is essentially an alternate form of the pretest. For each objective within the unit, there is a curriculum-embedded test that is part of the instructional sequence. These curriculum-embedded tests not only measure performance on the objective on which the student has been working, but also include test exercises on the next objective on which the student is likely to work. The notion here is that if a lesson is taught well, the student will learn not only the present lesson, but will be able to master exercises in the immediately subsequent skill. It is a special challenge for those who write lessons to make this "testing out" of an objective as frequent an occurrence as possible.

At the beginning of a school year, a student takes one or more wide-band placement tests that consist of sample items measuring his mastery of the objectives of each of the units within a level of work. On the basis of his previous year's performance, an approximation is made of the student's level of achievement, and testing begins from there. The student is tested over a range from what he knows to what he has not yet learned. Depending on his background, and depending to some extent on how hierarchical the objectives of achievement in a subject matter are, the student's performance may be more or less cumulative.

Tests are seen as part of instruction. Students look forward to them because they get immediate information about whether they need additional work in a unit or can move on to new material. The overall philosophy of the built-in testing program is that the student's performance is monitored so as to have a detailed assessment of his performance and progress always available. The continuous recording and updating of these performance data seem to make special testing procedures unnecessary. As we improve in our ability to design a curriculum that adapts to individual differences, we suspect that the test-taking aspects generally present in education will diminish, as perhaps will the text-anxious or test-sensitive student.

As a student progresses through the units in the mathematics curriculum, a posttest mastery criterion of 85 percent is employed; that is, a student must achieve this level of performance before he moves on to the next unit. The setting of a criterion level, however, is an experimental question that is being investigated. Assuming a reasonably cumulative curriculum where new learning depends upon previous learning, do different units and differing students require a uniform level of proficiency? If too high a criterion is set, a student can spend too much time mastering fine points of one unit, while he might be beginning the next. A bright student might begin to learn multiplication while still becoming proficient in the fundamentals of addition and subtraction and in this way develop a richer concept of addition; another student may require more detailed mastery of fundamentals before he moves on.

Data Management

The accumulation and maintenance of the day-to-day records required for individualized instruction are a sizable enterprise for a school. In our first years at Oakleaf, we accomplished this by hand. Each teacher had the assistance of an aide for individualized classes. There was a data-processing room with a staff of clerks who received information from teachers and teacher assistants, processed it, and returned it to the classroom. After using this simulated computer system for two years, we designed an initial computerized data-processing system. In cooperation with the General Learning Corporation, a computer-management system was investigated. The particularly challenging research aspect of a computer-management system is the task of matching relevant measures of student performance with appropriate curriculum methods and materials to provide the teacher with assistance in preparing instructional prescriptions for each student.

Learning and Teaching

A system for adapting to individual differences requires more than specification of objectives, measurement and assessment of these objectives, and the monitoring of student performance and progress. It also requires learning and teaching. The primary task to be faced here is that instruction involves teaching the student and not the classroom group. This has created a problem for many teachers who were trained to teach a class and have had much less experience in teaching individuals. Moreover, instructional materials, especially in the elementary school, are designed to be used with groups rather than with individuals.

Adapting instructional materials and procedures to individual differences is a function of both the behavior of the student and the nature of the subject matter being taught. It is important to emphasize at this point that individualization is accomplished by designing a particular curriculum for the needs of a student. (The word "needs" is used operationally in terms of student characteristics that we can reliably assess and that are relevant to instructional decisions.) Adapting to individual requirements does not at all imply that a student necessarily works alone or in any particular mode or setting. In the course of individualized instruction, students may be taught by lecture, by workbooks, by group discussion, by group projects, or by teaching machines. The essential notion is that individual requirements are matched to appropriate instructional procedures. Perhaps the term "individualized progress" is less misleading in this regard than the term "individualized instruction."

Patterns of Student Progress

What patterns of student progress occur under a system of individualized instruction? Figures 4-1 to 4-4 present computer-plotted summary charts that show the progress of different students in the mathematics curriculum at the Oakleaf School over a three-year period. In Figure 4-1 the vertical axis on the left-hand side lists the numbers of the curriculum units. There are eighty-eight units in the curriculum sequence; on each chart, these unit numbers may or may not begin at one or end at eighty-eight, depending on the level and unit at which the student originally placed. General descriptions of sets of units are given along this axis to show what the student is working on. For example, around the fortieth unit, a student would be working on beginning multiplication and division algorithms and on equivalent fractions. The vertical axis on the right-hand side shows the same thing, but lists the levels A through E and the names of the units in the level. These letters roughly correspond to material covered in standard textbooks: A is kindergarten, B is first-year work, C is second-year work, D is third and fourth year, E is fourth and fifth, F is fifth and sixth, and G is sixth and above. On the horizontal axis, units that are mastered during a particular two-week period over the three years of school are plotted. Every time a unit is mastered, an X is plotted. The Xs represent a rather stringent mastery criterion of 85 percent, and are only plotted on this chart if such a mastery level has been attained either on a unit posttest or a pretest. An X is also plotted when a student requires review and repeats some work in a unit in order to reattain proficiency. Teachers use the 85 percent mastery criterion as a basis for prescribing new work; sometimes, however, they decide that a student should be permitted to go on without insisting that he meet this criterion, but this is not shown here. The number of units mastered is one measure of student rate through the curriculum, although units differ widely in the average time required to work through them. The average time to master a unit was twelve days with a range of one to sixty days, one day representing pretest mastery. In Figures 4-1 to 4-4 the patterns of Xs

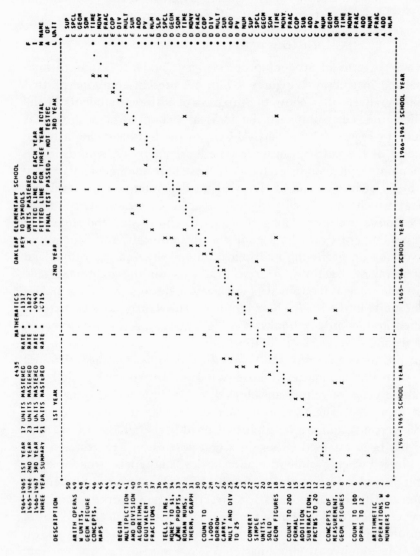

Figure 4-1
Janie

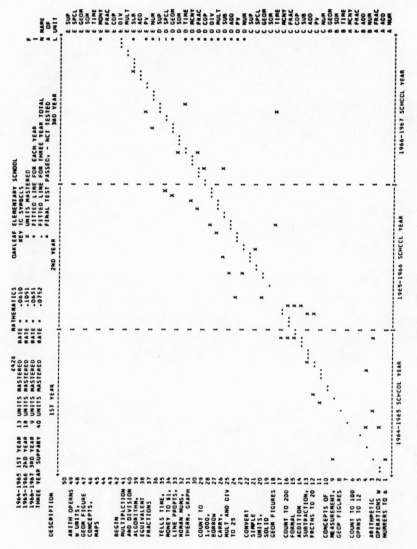

Figure 4-2
Leonard

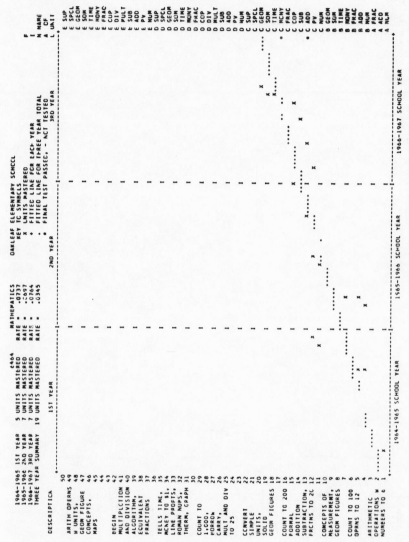

Figure 4-3
Jimmy

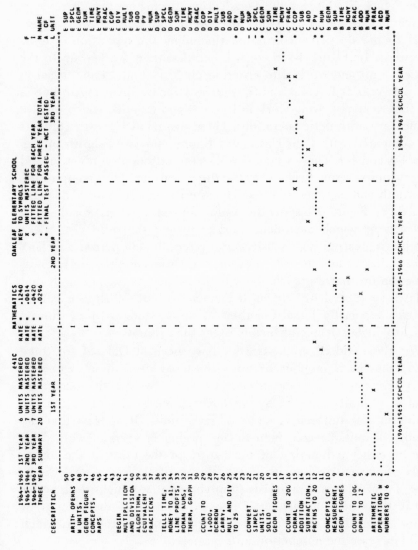

Figure 4-4
Joey

show how achievement progresses for different students. The straight line of dots on the chart represents a linear least squares fit of the Xs to show a general progress rate over three years.

In Figure 4-1, Janie, a third grader, has, during her first three years of school, worked up to the forty-sixth and worked on fifty-one units to the 85 percent criterion (including the repetition of units reviewed). In Figure 4-2, Leonard, her classmate, worked up to the fortieth unit and worked to criterion on forty units. Janie began in the first year at levels B and C, whereas Leonard spent much time in his first year reviewing work in levels A and early B, which involve elementary arithmetic operations. These two relatively swift students are compared with their classmates Jimmy and Joey, shown in Figures 4-3 and 4-4. These students worked to criterion on nineteen and twenty units, respectively, over the three years and worked up to the twentieth and eighteenth units. The asterisks on the right-hand vertical axis of Figure 4-1 show the result of a test, prepared for the level or levels at which a student worked during the third year. Each asterisk represents high mastery and retention—85 percent; a blank space indicates less than 85 percent; a dash means that the test was not given on that unit. When one looks at the asterisks, he finds that the two swift students shown in Figures 4-1 and 4-2 show excellent mastery, especially Janie. For the two slower students, Joey showed a slightly higher degree of final mastery than Jimmy.

For the hundred students who have been at Oakleaf for three years, the mean number of units mastered over these years was thirty-seven with a standard deviation of twelve; the maximum number of units covered by a student was seventy-three, and the minimum was thirteen, a range of sixty units. It appears that the number of units covered increases in the higher years of work. This may be either a function of the nature of the units at the higher levels of the curriculum or of the ability of the older students to move faster with our materials (implying that we might do a better job at the earlier levels), or it may be a result of the amount of review assigned by the teachers at the beginning of the year, which would increase the number of units mastered.

One indication of the consistency of the rate with which a student moves through the mathematics curriculum is given by the correlation of the number of units covered in the different years of the program. The three intercorrelations between the first, second, and third years are .37 (1 versus 2), .45 (2 versus 3), and .52 (1 versus 3). These are not as high as one would expect. The correlation between the knowledge that a student brings with him at the beginning of his first year—that is, where he places and begins in the curriculum—and the number of units he covers over three years was .61. This relationship is also reflected by a correlation of .72 between the number of the unit begun in the first year with the number of the unit reached at the end of the third year. The correlation between the rough measure of intelligence used by the school system (the California Test of Mental Maturity) and total number of units covered over three years was .32; similarly, the correlation between intelligence and the number of the unit reached at the end of the third year was .31.

It appears that the first phase of individually prescribed instruction provides a start toward individualizing certain aspects of a school curriculum—a start that can be specifically studied, revised, and improved. We are encouraged now to investigate intensively the relationships and the conditions of learning that underlie the attainment of a broad spectrum of educational goals. It is conceivable that individualized instruction will find its major value in attaining not only achievement objectives but other educational goals such as self-direction, self-initiation of one's learning, and the feeling of control over one's learning environment, although success in reaching these outcomes of learning is difficult to measure. Progress in the design of systems for the individualization of instruction can only be seriously considered if we try to understand the relationships that underlie the practices we implement. Neither we, nor anyone else, will have any significant or reliable success with a program of individualized instruction unless such understanding is obtained by sustained research, development, and experimentation in the schools. An example of careful development is exemplified by the New Primary Grades Reading System.

The New Primary Grades Reading System (NRS)

This example of sustained development at LRDC is an individualized reading program developed and directed by Isabel Beck and is currently undergoing classroom tryouts in two developmental schools.[7]

NRS is an individualized system that permits children to progress at various rates, allows for different routes to the mastery of an objective, and is organized so that a teacher can monitor a classroom of children doing different things at different times. The system is adaptive to the needs of individuals by means of alternative teaching strategies and opportunities for student self-direction. The system, designed to encompass the domain traditionally covered by the first three years of reading instruction, is oriented toward urban children. Upon completion of the program, children are expected to be able to read and demonstrate an understanding of representative third-grade selections.

NRS uses a code-breaking approach to beginning reading—an eclectic phonic approach based on linguistic principles. It is phonic because many grapheme-phoneme relationships are taught directly and practiced in isolation; it is eclectic phonic because both synthetic phonics and analytic phonics are employed. The program is based on linguistic principles because words and texts are frequently displayed to maximize similarities and contrasts in major spelling patterns and because the teaching of explicit rules is kept at a minimum. There is also a strong commitment to having reading materials approximate natural syntax and structure as nearly as possible, which is based upon the assumption that the reading of meaningful units must be approached early in instruction.

Word attack skills are taught through correspondences of symbols and sounds, similar spelling patterns, contrasting spelling patterns, and whole words. The blending of symbol-sound correspondences is taught through a specifically designed algorithm based upon principles of synthetic phonics. It is a specific strategy for putting sounds together to form words. Mastery of this algorithm allows most children to attack new word combinations independently and successfully in the first week of instruction.

The program consists of sixteen levels, each containing about ten instructional sequences. As an illustration, Figure 4-5 shows the contents of Level III. To enable children to engage in reading situations that resemble real-world reading situations, NRS designers have developed three categories of materials. The first, the prescriptive category, is essentially controlled by the teacher. The second, the student selection category, affords the student the opportunity to select activity A or activity B. And the third, the choice category, arranged by level rather than by sequence, allows the child to choose from a variety of materials and activities.

Sequence	Symbol-sound correspondences	Sight words	Spelling patterns	Comprehension formats	Stories	Tests
1	ch - *ch*in					Progress check
2	o - *on*		op, ot	Multiple choice with three alternatives		Progress check
3	l - *l*ap	and				Progress check
4			et, it, ot, ap, ip, op			Criterion test
5					Group story	
6	r - *r*an	to				Progress check
7			ell, ill	Follows printed directions		Progress check
8	g - *g*et	of				Progress check
9	h - *h*am					Progress check
10			ag, eg, og, ig			Criterion test
11	or - *for*					Progress check
12					Group story	Criterion test

Figure 4-5
Content of NRS Level III

A discussion of the activities and the movement of a student through the sequence can show how the three situations occur in NRS. A flow chart of one instructional sequence from Level VI is presented in Figure 4-6. This diagram indicates that the student begins the sequence with a cassette-led lesson designated A, follows with the correlated A-form workbook exercises, and then interacts with the teacher on a progress check. If his performance is satisfactory, the student leaves the prescriptive situation and selects his next activity from the two possibilities at his level. In the sample given in Figure 4-6, his choice is to read Story 2, a Creek Indian legend, or Story 5, a collection of riddles. Both activities require the child to answer questions about what he chose to read, and both incorporate the new content introduced in the prescriptive materials just encountered, while cumulatively maintaining earlier content.

If the student's performance is not satisfactory, the teacher will prescribe the cassette-led lesson designated B. The B-form cassette and correlated workbook pages are essentially the same in instructional technique as the A-form, but provide another teaching instance using different examples. After the student completes the B-form exercises, the teacher administers Progress Check B. Once again, if performance is satisfactory on the check, the student then selects his next activity. But, if performance is unsatisfactory, the teacher must choose one of two prescriptions. One possible choice is to recycle the student through the A-form material again. Because time has passed since the student first performed the A material, this may not seem as repetitious as an immediate recycle. The other possible prescription that the teacher may make is to enter the child into alternative teaching strategies. When the student performs satisfactorily on Progress Check B, he will return to the selection of either Story 2 or Story 5 as his next activity.

When the student completes the activity he selected, he enters the third situation, his own choice. As shown on the chart, the student decides if he wants to perform some of the horizontal activities or move on to the next new instruction. If he decides to proceed to the new instruction, he will move through a basically similar procedure of teacher prescription and student selection. If the student chooses to remain at his current level, he will choose from many activities. Children's decisions, at such points, help to determine how fast some children get through the program. It may well be that one child exits later than another because he decided to do more things, not because he learned more slowly.

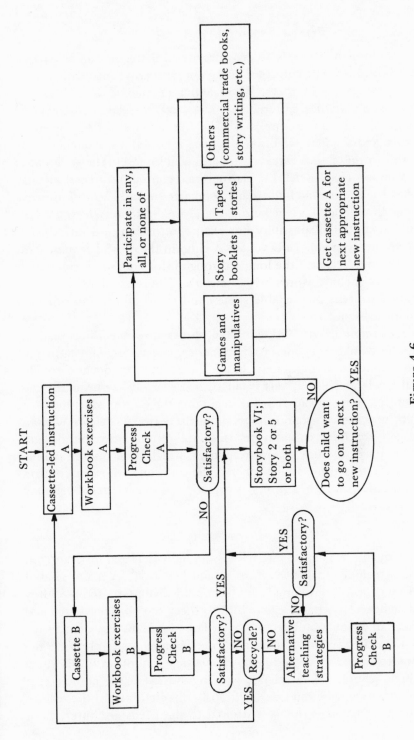

Figure 4-6
Flow chart of the NRS instructional sequence

In the third situation, NRS provides varied materials and activities, giving the student the choice of doing one of them, some of them, all of them, or none of them. These activities include NRS-designed games, manipulatables, and story booklets, and correlated commercial trade books and taped stories. Unlike the activities of teacher prescription and student selection that are arranged by sequence, the activities in the choice category are arranged by level. The games and stories in any level use all the instructional content up to and including that level. Since a child in any sequence in Level VI can use any game or book coded VI or below, therefore, "discovery learning" of upcoming content is possible. For example, the long *o* is introduced in the seventh sequence of Level VI. A child in the second sequence of Level VI could "learn" the long *o* through informal use of games and stories that include words with long *o*'s. This sort of exposure to upcoming content may enable some children to pretest out of some instructional sequences.

The example given in Figure 4-6 shows how the three reading situations combine in one instructional sequence. Similar opportunities for children to participate in the three situations occur throughout all levels of NRS. Levels I and II, however, utilize primarily the prescriptive route because, in the beginning stages of reading in NRS, concern is centered around the relationship between oral and written language. Teaching children to translate letters into sounds and words requires the use of oral responses, which then require confirmation. At this time, the teacher is the only one who can confirm oral responses, and, therefore, her prescriptive role in these beginning stages is crucial.

Individualized Science (IS)

Individualized Science, like NRS, is an individualized program, but it adapts to individual differences in another way.[8] A major goal of IS, which was developed by Leopold Klopfer and Audrey Champagne, is to enable each child to meet the challenges of rapid advances in science and technology. The aim is no less than to develop a completely individualized science learning system to serve the student from the time he begins elementary school up to his entry into high school. For a science learning system to be complete, it must be consciously and conscientiously directed toward the realization of a set of goals that are attuned to the needs and interests of the student, to the development of the child, and to the circumstances of the 1970s. Such a set of goals has been identified for this program.

The first goal is one of self-direction by the student in which he views the learning process as primarily self-directed and self-initiated. The second goal is one of coevaluation by the student in which he plays a major role in evaluating the quality, extent, and rapidity of his learning. The third is the affective goal in which the student displays positive attitudes toward his study of science, scientific inquiry, and the scientific enterprise. Inquiry is the fourth goal, in which the student is skillful in using the processes of scientific inquiry and is also able to carry out specific inquiries. And, the fifth is the goal of scientific literacy in which the student acquires a foundation of scientific literacy.

These goals represent a kind of composite description of a student near the end of the IS program. The student's attainment of any or all of these goals is, of course, a developmental process. We assume that there are identifiable levels in the student's development toward the attainment of the desired goals. We also assume that it is possible to specify most of the student's behaviors related to these five goals at each developmental level in terms of behavioral objectives. Clear and comprehensive specification of objectives is a vital part of an effective individualized learning system.

There are ten levels of student development in IS. In the first three levels the child is introduced to various processes of scientific inquiry and has many opportunities to sharpen skills in using these processes as he explores several different areas of science. In the next four levels, corresponding approximately to the intermediate grades, the main focus is on the child's application of his process skills in problem solving and on his accumulation of knowledge and understanding about himself and his environment. In the last three levels the child carries out genuine investigations, that is, inquiries where the answers are not known. He utilizes his process skills and existing knowledge to acquire new concepts, principles, and insights.

Learning Resources

While it is comforting to have a set of goals and a framework of developmental levels, provisions must obviously be made for suitable and varied means of attaining the several goals of IS. The various types of learning resources available to the student at different levels of IS are listed in Table 4-1, which also indicates the learning resources that contribute to the attainment of each of the five goals. All these learning resources are not used at every level of IS. Just as the student grows and changes, so too the learning resources available to him must reflect growth and change. Thus, for example, mini-explorations and student activities are replaced by invitations to explore, and directed group activities change into student seminars. Some learning resources, however, are available throughout all levels of development (for example, science learning games), though their degree of sophistication may change.

To make it possible for a student to progress toward the attainment of the goals of self-direction and coevaluation, learning resources must be available from which he may select numerous

Table 4-1

Learning resources that contribute to the goals of IS

| Learning resources | Goals | | | | |
	Student self-direction	Student co-evaluation	Affective	Inquiry	Scientific literacy
Individual lesson		X		X	X
Individual taped lesson				X	X
Men and ideas filmstrip			X		X
Miniexploration	X	X	X	X	X
Readings in science		X	X		X
Directed group activity			X	X	X
Student seminar		X	X	X	X
Student activity	X	X	X	X	X
Invitation to explore	X	X	X	X	X
Self-initiated independent activity	X	X	X	X	X
Science learning game			X	X	X
Science notebook	X	X		X	X
Planning booklet	X	X			
Keys book	X	X			
"How to . . ." booklet	X			X	

alternatives for his study or investigation. In addition, the expectations for completion of an activity or the standards for judging mastery of a unit of study must be known to the student, so that he may participate intelligently in evaluating his performance. Learning resources having both these characteristics include student activities, invitations to explore, self-initiated independent activities, miniexplorations, and mini-investigations. Individual prescriptions also contribute to the goals of self-direction and coevaluation. In the beginning of IS, prescriptions are prepared by the teacher, but the student is increasingly encouraged to write his own prescriptions as he progresses through the levels. Finally, the system of guidance and selection, which operates on the last eight levels, is intended to advise and assist the student in directing and evaluating his own learning.

To make possible the implementation of the affective and inquiry goals, it is mandatory to have learning resources that provide some enjoyable experiences for the student in which he can be successful and that offer opportunities for the development of inquiry skills and for abundant practice in inquiry. One indication of the determination about enabling the student to reach the affective and inquiry goals is that all but two of the resources used in IS directly contribute to the attainment of one or both of these goals, as Table 4-1 shows.

To fulfill such an inquiry goal, a science program must provide the student with instruction in basic skills of scientific inquiry. It must also provide instruction that will make it possible for him to acquire the necessary information to carry out an investigation in an area of science of his own choosing. Equally as important as skills and information are a favorable attitude toward inquiry and the availability of opportunities to practice scientific inquiry. The learning resources of IS provide the student with the instruction by which he can learn the basic skills and information, experiences that are conducive to the development of positive attitudes toward scientific inquiry, and many opportunities to engage in inquiries on a level appropriate to his development. Taped and written lessons, done individually by the child, provide instruction in skills and information. Science learning games and the men and ideas filmstrip series are especially designed to instill positive attitudes toward the study of science and scientific inquiry. Miniexplorations provide the child with opportunities to integrate skills, information, and attitudes acquired from the other learning resources into elementary inquiry-type experiences. Directed group activities and seminars enable the child to share the results of his inquiries with other children and to get feedback on his results from them.

Contributions to the attainment of the goal of scientific literacy are also made by almost all our learning resources. This is hardly surprising since the locus for most of the program's subject-matter content is in the goal of scientific literacy, and learning resources normally deal with some science content.

The main theme for organizing content in IS is the pervasive notion of systems. In the third through seventh levels the following organizing theme for the science content is used: "People and Their Systems: Natural Living Systems, Natural Nonliving Systems, and Man-Made Systems. Man can think about the natural world as a nested hierarchy of systems and subsystems. Some natural systems are living systems and some are nonliving systems. People themselves are a living system with interacting subsystems. And, people create new systems, in which they may be participants, and which they can control."[9] The units of these levels focus on, first, man as a living system and, second, the systems that man creates, controls, conceives, and studies.

The student's varied experiences with many types of systems lead into semi-independent inquiries in the eighth to tenth levels. Here the following organizing theme for the science content is used: "The Biosphere: Ecosystem of the Earth. The biosphere is the thin envelope near the earth's surface where all known living systems normally exist. It is a global ecosystem where natural living systems, including man, interact with each other and with natural nonliving systems, and where man-made systems interact with natural systems and with each other."[10] In the units and investigations of the eighth through tenth levels, the content emphasis is primarily on the small-scale and large-scale equilibriums in the environment, between the environment and living organisms, and among living organisms. In these units many of the social problems in which science is a sizable component come into consideration. From experiences in the last three levels of IS the student should come to understand and to value the ecosystem in which he lives and to know what he must do to survive in it.

Mainstream and Alternative Pathways

Implicit in the discussion up to this point has been our commitment to individualization, but the organizing notion relating to individualization remains to be made explicit. One type of individualization provided for in IS is the rate at which the student progresses. This means that each student can progress at a rate adapted to his individual learning style, which is dependent upon how rapidly he masters successive units on a learning continuum. We use this feature in the part of IS called the mainstream, the common core of scientific learning in which every student is expected to achieve mastery. Units of study in the mainstream are arranged in a sequence. For example, there are five mainstream units on the fifth and sixth levels. Each unit is identified by the name of a scientist who made some contribution to the field of science with which that particular unit concerns itself. Thus, the Voit Unit is concerned with human nutrition, the Joule Unit with the concept of energy, the Beaumont Unit with the processes of digestion, the Powell Unit with the role of water in natural systems, and the Harvey Unit with the circulation of blood.

There is a continuum of five mainstream units that a student may choose to interrupt at any time by selecting one or several of the activities in alternative pathways. Each of these alternative units arise from possible points of curiosity on the student's part or his desire to know more about topics covered in the mainstream units.

The notion of mainstream and alternative pathways is used throughout IS. As the student progresses, he has continually increasing opportunities to select learning experiences in diverse and meaningful alternative pathways. By providing resources in both mainstream and alternative pathways to meet the needs and interests of the student, we expect that IS will not only be individualized, but will also be relevant to scientific and technological advances made in our society.

Instructional Programs Designed to Improve Entering Abilities

As indicated, an adaptive instructional system is designed to improve certain skills that seem necessary for continued success in school. The Primary Education Project (PEP), under the direction of Lauren Resnick and Margaret Wang, was a preschool and kindergarten extension of the elementary school instructional programs that were being developed at LRDC. Fundamental to the design of the PEP program was its emphasis on the detailed analysis of preschool cognitive tasks and on the development of hierarchically ordered prerequisites for learning. One of the components of PEP, as originally conceived, was a section devoted to perceptual skills which, in time, under the direction of Jerome Rosner, assumed a separate identity as the Perceptual Skills Curriculum. Both PEP and the Perceptual Skills Curriculum are discussed in this section.

Beginning Concepts: PEP

In 1967 PEP was introduced in a second developmental public school, the Frick School in Pittsburgh. Here we were able to work in a different socioeconomic environment and with younger children. PEP, designed for three- and four-year-olds and begun at Frick, has recently been described as follows.[11]

It has been widely observed that children who begin school at a relative disadvantage tend to fall increasingly further behind their more advantaged peers as they progress through the school grades. A possible reason for this phenomenon of "cumulative deficit" lies in the failure of certain children to have mastered critical prerequisites for early school performance. As a result, they fail to master the material of the first year's curriculum. Since this material is, in turn, prerequisite to the next year's learning, they continue at a disadvantage into the following year. As unmastered prerequisites accumulate through successive years of school, the negative prognosis for school success increases. If this analysis is correct, then a strategy for breaking the cumulative deprivation cycle would need to begin very early to establish the prerequisites of school performance and to assure that each child masters each succeeding set of objectives before proceeding to higher levels of instruction.

PEP has been concerned with the development and evaluation of a model of early education that would meet these aims within the context of a program concerned with the child's general cognitive and social growth. The program was developed so that the preschool would indeed prepare children for successful mastery of the academic work of the primary grades, but in a primary grade environment that itself respected the best principles that could be called upon concerning how children learned and how teaching should proceed. While PEP can be used in places where a traditional or a very different kind of reformed primary grade education is in store for the children, it has been conceived as part of a continuum—reflecting an assumption that basic strategies of learning and basic principles of teaching undergo no radical change at the end of what is institutionally labeled "preschool." The process of breaking the cycle of cumulative deficit can begin in the preschool, but it cannot end there. The preschool program must, rather, be integrated with an equally powerful primary school program if maximum effects are to be realized.

Theoretical Foundations

The primary question concerned an environment for learning to learn: could an environment be created that would maximize the learning abilities and motivational tendencies of children from all kinds of home backgrounds? It was necessary to design an early learning program that was explicitly intended to teach children the skills and concepts that underlie intelligent school performance and that was adaptive to individual differences in manner and rate of learning. Developmental work over several years has been aimed at providing a school environment that meets two essential requirements. First, the school must assure an atmosphere in which children can become confident of their own ability to learn and to cope with their surroundings. Second, it must help the children to become truly effective at learning, at coping with problems, and at meeting real demands. Self-confidence based on an artificial lowering of all demands and expectations would, likely, evaporate as soon as the child moved out of the protected environment; only true competence would breed confidence that lasted beyond the school yard or the years of the special program.

These requirements called for a school environment in which the child experienced much success, and in which momentary difficulty with some task was not interpreted as failure by either teacher or child. These requirements also called for an environment in which children had sufficient freedom, both in moving about their physical surroundings and in choosing activities for themselves, to become capable of significantly controlling their own learning and social activities. Finally, they dictated an environment in which the child was expected to be able to learn, that consistently communicated this expectation to him, and that arranged instruction so that, in fact, the child could and did learn most of the time. It is precisely this kind of adaptive early learning environment that PEP seeks to provide for preschool children.

There is wide agreement among psychologists that cognitive development proceeds in ordered and essentially "hierarchical" fashion.

This implies that certain abilities quite uniformly appear earlier than others and that those abilities are, in some sense, the "prerequisites" for the acquisition of more complex abilities. This hierarchically ordered characterization of cognitive development is shared by psychologists who differ widely in other respects. It underlies notions of "stages of cognitive development" in Piagetian and related theory,[12] and it is also the basis for the theory of "cumulative learning" proposed by Gagné and others whose theory underlies much of the behaviorally oriented work in instruction.[13]

These two approaches, normally considered as opposite and competing theories regarding cognitive development and instruction, share a belief in the mutually interactive role of organismic and environmental events in the development of cognitive competence; they differ largely in emphasis. Piagetians stress the natural and universal sequence of development and the role of "general experience" in providing the child with events that eventually force cognitive "accommodation" or the development of new cognitive structures.[14] Cumulative learning theory attempts to break "general experience" apart, proposing that certain of the events comprising it are probably the most critical and powerful. Thus, once these are identified, direct and positive steps can be taken to influence cognitive development by providing instructional experiences that "match" current states of competence not only in general ways but in ways that are highly specific, and thus maximally effective in producing cognitive change.[15]

PEP has assumed the possibility of making these specific matches and has thus espoused a form of cumulative learning theory as a guideline for generating curriculum. At the same time it has accepted as its goal the development of generalized rather than specific abilities and thus shares with Piagetian and other cognitive theorists a concern for general concepts and learning abilities.

Research Foundations

In the 1960s proposals for preschool programs of different kinds were largely derived from general theoretical positions and, occasionally, from short-term laboratory studies. As development of the PEP program began, it was necessary to be more concerned with building into the developmental work itself an active program of research and formative evaluation.

Three general classes of skills were identified for inclusion in PEP's early learning curriculum.[16] The first are perceptual-motor skills. These skills, which generally are considered to underlie conceptual functioning of a higher order, include the ability to use one's body efficiently and be aware of its position in space, as well as to make a wide range of sensory discriminations. Conceptual-linguistic skills constitute the second class, which includes such skills as classification, reasoning, memory, and early mathematics, together with the language facility that supports and gives expression to competence in these areas. The third class, orienting and attending skills, includes the ability to concentrate on a task and resist distractions; the ability to attend to appropriate details; to follow directions; to control impulses and accept rewards that are delayed rather than immediate and verbal rather than concrete. Also included are those abilities that are usually discussed as motivational traits: confidence in one's ability to succeed and willingness to attempt new tasks; persistence in working on a task even in the face of frustration or distraction; a tendency to complete tasks rather than abandon them before they are finished; and pride in accomplishment. Related to these traits are certain social skills, such as accepting and giving help, that together with the others just mentioned permit a child to function well in a classroom and to learn from the environment.

Orienting and attending skills are, in a sense, prerequisite to all the other skills in an early learning program. For some children, a relatively long period of attention to these skills alone may be required. In any case, a preschool program that ignores the need to develop and nurture these adaptive behaviors will almost certain fail in its attempt to develop skills of a higher order and concepts for all children.

PEP's work in curriculum development began by identifying, for each curriculum area, a fairly extended set of specific abilities which taken together would constitute an acceptable level of cognitive competence for a six- or seven-year-old child. The preschool curriculum was developed by working backward from these goals to identify prerequisites and sequences of learning tasks that would maximize correspondence with natural sequences of acquisition and that would maximize transfer. Once a set of target tasks was identified, it was necessary to begin to hypothesize the actual steps involved in skilled performance of the task.

One of the first curricula to be established was the Quantification

Curriculum. It is an introductory mathematics curriculum intended to teach fundamental concepts and operations in forms simple enough to be learned by every preschool child yet broad enough to serve as a conceptual foundation for later work. Number is the core concept around which this curriculum is organized.

The first step in developing a hierarchy of curriculum objectives leading to an operational concept of number was to specify in behavioral terms a set of specific components of the number concept. The behaviors thus specified comprise an operational definition of the number concept in the form of concrete performances, which, *taken together*, permit the inference that the child has an abstract concept of "number."

A listing of objectives as in Table 4-2 appears to suggest a fixed and linear path of learning for all children. Such a suggestion is not intended. Rather, the objectives are organized into complex hierarchies that permit multiple paths while still respecting fundamental prerequisite relations among objectives. Hierarchical relationships among objectives within the units are demonstrated in Figure 4-7, while Figure 4-8 shows the pattern of relationship between the units.

The PEP Classification Curriculum is part of an extended program in reasoning and related language abilities that will eventually extend through approximately the second grade. Several instructional units dealing with basic matching, sorting, and labeling skills have been extensively tested in preschool and kindergarten classrooms. They form the present preschool curriculum, in which early matching and classifying activities lead the child to recognize the features used in the school culture for grouping of objects. Throughout the curriculum, labeling and descriptive activities built into most objectives lead to increasing skill in verbal communication and verbal mediation.

The instructional objectives of the curriculum are organized into nine units as shown in Figure 4-9. Table 4-3 gives the specific objectives for each unit.

Organization of Content: The Preschool Learning Environment

Given the complexity of content discussed above, and given the central concern for adaptation to individual differences, PEP was faced with a major task of organizing the classroom and teaching program in a form manageable for young children. As stated, one major goal of PEP is the development of what are termed orienting and attending skills. They include both the general abilities to manage one's own activities in a relatively complex environment and the specific attentional skills that allow children to focus on relevant details of learning tasks, to persist at a task, to resist irrelevant distractions, and the like. These abilities are, as indicated, prerequisites to learning activities of all kinds and at all levels of development. They are, however, less amenable to sequential programming of the kind represented in the Quantification and Classification Curricula. Rather, abilities of this kind develop in response to general environmental conditions.

Environments that demand and make possible self-management and planning skills will foster the development of such skills. Similarly, successions of tasks that require increasing persistence, patience, and attention to detail ought to result in the development of these characteristics, particularly if the environment is responsive, reacting positively to small successes and gradually making more complex demands. An overriding objective in designing the PEP classroom was to provide an environment that would develop and support adaptive orienting and attending skills in young children.

A second major objective was to provide a system of diagnosis and assessment that would allow teachers to adapt the program to individual needs. This meant, at a minimum, assuring that children were neither required to repeat tasks they already mastered nor expected to work on objectives for which they lacked critical prerequisites.

These general objectives dictated the broad outlines of the PEP preschool environment. They demanded, first, a system in which teachers could keep track of children's developing capabilities—a demand met through a combination of tests keyed to the structured curriculum objectives and informal observation of the children. They also demanded a system for displaying learning materials in such a way that children could both find them and return them to their place on their own. This would minimize "housekeeping" problems for teachers, but, even more importantly, would serve to develop the children's sense of responsibility for their physical environment and their self-management skills. Finally, a method was required for guiding children in selection of materials and activities. In certain exploratory portions of the program this meant, in the main, keeping down "crowding," and the resultant competition and chaos, by

Table 4-2
Objectives of the Quantification Curriculum

Units	Given:	The child can:
Units 1 and 2 (counting and one-to-one correspondence[a])	A. Sets of up to five objects or up to ten objects B. Set of movable objects C. Fixed ordered set of objects D. Fixed unordered set of objects E. A numeral stated and a set of objects F. A numeral stated and several sets of fixed objects G. Two sets of objects H. Two unequal sets of objects I. Two unequal sets of objects	A. Recite the numerals in order B. Count the objects, moving them out of the set as he counts C. Count the objects D. Count the objects E. Count out a subset of stated size F. Select a set of size indicated by numeral G. Pair objects and state whether the sets are equivalent H. Pair objects and state which set has more I. Pair objects and state which set has less
Units 3 and 4 (numerals[b])	A. Two sets of numerals B. A numeral stated, and a set of printed numerals C. A numeral (written) D. Several sets of objects and several numerals E. Two numerals (written) F. A set of numerals G. Numerals stated	A. Match the numerals B. Select the stated numeral C. Read the numeral D. Match numerals with appropriate sets E. State which shows more (less) F. Place them in order G. Write the numeral
Unit 5 (comparison of sets)	A. Two sets of objects B. Two sets of objects C. A set of objects and a numeral D. A numeral and several sets of objects E. Two rows of objects (not paired) F. Three sets of objects	A. Count sets and state which has more objects or that sets have same number B. Count sets and state which has fewer objects C. State which shows more (less) D. Select sets that are more (less) than the numeral; given a set of objects and several numerals, the child can select numerals that show more (less) than the set of objects

Unit 6
(seriation and ordinal
position)

E. State which row has more regardless of arrangement
F. Count sets and state which has most (least)

A. Three objects of different sizes
B. Objects of graduated sizes
C. Several sets of objects
D. Ordered set of objects

A. Select the largest (smallest)
B. Seriate according to size
C. Seriate sets according to size
D. Name the ordinal position of the objects

Unit 7
(addition and subtraction
[sums to 10])

A. Two numbers stated, set of objects, and
directions to add
B. Two numbers stated, set of objects and
directions to subtract
C. Two numbers stated, number line, and
directions to add
D. Two numbers stated, number line, and
directions to subtract
E. Addition and subtraction word problems
F. Written addition and subtraction problems
in form: x or x

$+y$ $-y$

G. Addition and subtraction problems in form:
x + y = or x − y =

A. Add the numbers by counting out two subsets
then combining and stating combined number
as sum
B. Count out smaller subset from larger and state
remainder
C. Use number line to determine sum
D. Use number line to subtract
E. Solve the problems
F. Complete the problems
G. Complete the equations

[a]Unit 1 involves sets of up to five objects; unit 2 involves sets of up to ten objects.
[b]Unit 3 involves numerals and sets of up to five objects; unit 4 involves numerals and sets of up to ten objects.

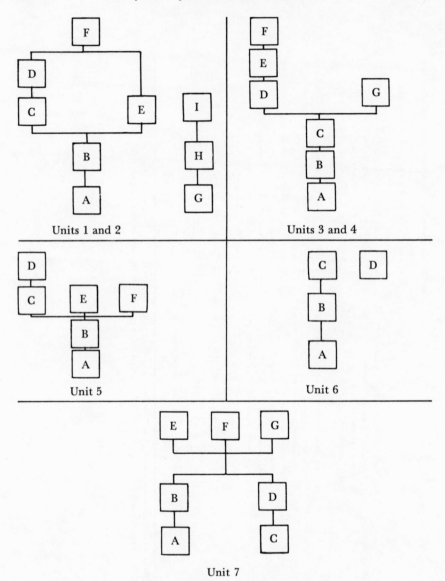

Figure 4-7
Hierarchical relations within PEP Quantification units

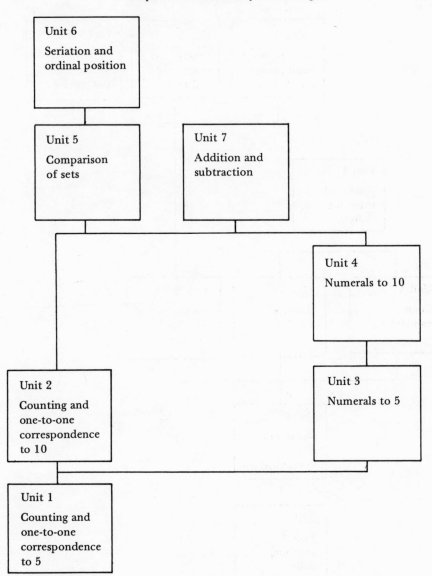

Figure 4-8
Hierarchical relations between PEP Quantification units

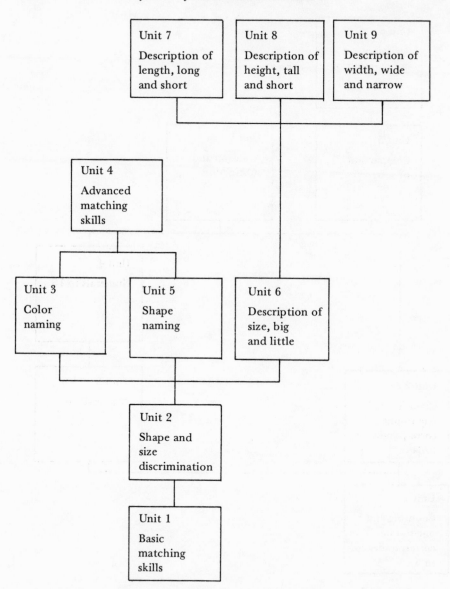

Figure 4-9
Hierarchical relations between PEP Classification units

limiting the number of children using any particular area at one time. With respect to the prescriptive portions of the program, it meant developing a manageable strategy for telling each child what specific objectives and activities in the curriculum he was to work on each day.

There was an attempt throughout to maintain as much flexibility as possible with respect to the particular instructional materials used, while at the same time the teachers were provided with adequate guidance concerning effective materials and how to use them. This flexibility was viewed as important mainly because it served to maintain an open educational system—one that could absorb new instructional strategies as teachers learned about them and that could reject those that were not working for particular teachers or particular groups of children. In addition, flexibility with respect to the specific teaching materials provides an important degree of economic adaptability, since schools adopting PEP can usually adapt equipment and materials already on hand to the new program, rather than discarding them entirely in favor of specified materials.

Diagnosis and Testing

The provision for individual diagnosis and monitoring of progress is at the core of PEP. Monitoring of progress was essential during the developmental stages of the project as a basis for revising and improving the program. It remains important as a means of providing teachers with the information necessary for adapting use of the components of the program to individual children and also for communicating on a substantive basis with parents and other adults concerned with the children's development. In PEP classrooms, this diagnosis and monitoring function is accomplished by a combination of informal observations the teacher makes while circulating among and working with the children, and the administration of special criterion-referenced tests keyed to the objectives in the various curricula.[17]

Once a child is socially comfortable in the classroom, and general routines are well established, the teacher or aide takes each child aside and begins the testing program. The first task is to find his "entering level." This is normally done by administering a special "placement test," composed of a sampling of items from the units. Children are rated as passing or failing each unit on the basis of this test. For units failed, tests on the individual objectives are then

Table 4-3
Objectives of the Classification Curriculum

Units	Given:	The child can:
Unit 1 (basic matching skills)	A. A set of two objects	A. State whether the pairs are the "same" or "different"
	B. Two identical sets of objects	B. Pair identical objects
	C. An array of objects varying in one dimension	C. Sort on the basis of differing attributes of that dimension
	D. Three objects—two identical, one different	D. Identify the one that is different
	E. A sample object and three dissimilar objects	E. Identify the one that matches the sample
Unit 2 (shape and size discrimination)	A. Basic shapes and matching outlines	A. Place the shapes on the appropriate outlines
	B. Irregular shapes and matching outlines	B. Place the shapes on the appropriate outlines
	C. Two sizes of rods and instructions to superimpose	C. State whether same or different size and give reason
	D. Two sizes of a shape and instructions to superimpose	D. State whether same or different and give reason
Unit 3 (color naming)	A. An array of the basic colors	A. Identify the stated colors
	B. An array of the basic colors	B. Name the colors
	C. Two identical sets of objects of different shades of a color	C. Match identical objects
	D. Several shades of a single color	D. Seriate in order from darkest to lightest

Unit 4
(shape naming)

A. An array of the seven basic shapes
B. An array of the seven basic shapes

A. Identify named shape
B. Name the shapes

Unit 5
(advanced matching skills)

A. Two objects, same on one dimension but different on another
B. Three objects, varying in three dimensions, two alike on a given dimension and one different on that given dimension
C. A sample object and a set of objects varying in two dimensions
D. An array of objects varying in two dimensions (color, shape, and size) and instructions to sort on the basis of one dimension

A. State whether the objects are the same or different and give reason
B. Identify the object that is different and give reason
C. Identify object that matches sample in one dimension and give reasons
D. Place objects in groups according to one dimension and explain the basis for the sort

Units 6-9
(big and little)

A. Two objects different in size
B. Two objects different in size
C. Two objects different in size
D. Two objects different in size
E. Two objects different in size
F. Two objects different in size
G. Several sizes of an object

A. Point to the "big" ("long," "tall," "wide") object
B. Verbally state which object is "big" etc. when asked
C. Identify the "little" ("short," "narrow") object
D. State which object is "little" etc. when asked
E. Describe according to size using the term "big" or "little" etc.
F. Compare and state which is "bigger," "smaller," etc.
G. Seriate in order from biggest to smallest

administered to determine exactly which objectives the child needs to work on. When a child does not pass a test, indicating that he needs work on a certain objective, he is given one or several "prescriptions," that is, assignments of activities relevant to learning that objective.

While test performance normally provides the occasion for advancing to new units in the curriculum, informal observations are at the heart of the day-to-day teaching and diagnosis. These observations are performed as the teacher works with children in exploratory and prescriptive tasks. Considerable work has been done to develop strategies of questioning that can serve both to help the teacher ascertain the child's conceptual level and to stretch the child's concepts through interaction. The observations made at the point of checking off the child's prescription ticket (a list of suggested activities) as he completes a prescribed task are of particular importance. Again, probing questions serve to extend both the teacher's knowledge of the child and the child's sense of his own competence.

Display of Materials and Choice of Activities

The requirement concerning the display of materials dictates the physical arrangements of the classroom. Materials for the various prescriptive curricula (Quantification, Classification, and parts of Perceptual Skills) are arranged in color- and number-coded boxes, each box containing the materials necessary for one instructional activity. These activities are intended for largely independent use by children, with the teacher circulating and helping, but not being present throughout an activity. The activities are directly keyed to the objectives of the curriculum. Several activities are normally keyed to each objective in order to allow maximum flexibility and adaptiveness to individual children.

In order to guide the use of these materials, the children are given "prescription tickets" before each session begins. Each child's ticket is made up daily on the basis of the teacher's observations and the results of recently administered tests. The tickets, which children quickly learn to find by themselves when they are displayed in a pocket chart in the classroom, contain codes that exactly match those on the boxes; the child then "follows" the ticket by finding a box whose code matches that on his ticket. The codes may direct the child to a particular activity, or they may be general and permit the child to choose one from a number of activities at a given level. The prescription system is, thus, both directive and flexible. The teacher can match it to her best judgments of the child's needs and capabilities. The child can be closely or loosely directed, again depending on the teacher's judgment.

The Perceptual Skills Curriculum

The importance of perceptual skills, originally an integral component of PEP, became apparent as initial research began to show direct and close relationships between certain of these skills and achievement in reading and mathematics. Continued investigations supported these early observations; thus the teaching of perceptual skills became sufficiently important to warrant a separate program, which became known as the Perceptual Skills Curriculum. The curriculum, under the direction of Jerome Rosner, continued to operate within the PEP model, but was used independently in other settings as well. The curriculum, now completed, is organized into four components, each dealing with a different subdomain of skills that have been shown to be directly linked in some way to classroom achievement.[18] These four are: Visual-Motor, Auditory-Motor, General-Motor, and Letters and Numerals. Each of the four components comprises a series of instructional goals—behavioral objectives—that are organized into a hierarchy of levels. Thus, each of the four is designed to allow for pretesting (to determine which levels of skill have already been mastered and which remain to be mastered) and posttesting (to determine when an instructional goal has been achieved). The curriculum also provides training activities for teaching these skills. Figures 4-10 and 4-11 are representative of the structure and progression of the programs.

The curriculum is based on three assumptions.

First, children enter school with some store of semantic and pictorial information. That is, they are able to code some amount of information as spatial images and/or as words. The principal functions of the primary grades are to foster the expansion and elaboration of this information and to teach children to code and decode the information with symbols—spoken words with letters, and spatial patterns with numerals.

Second, to perceive—in this context—involves the processes of analyzing spatial patterns and spoken words into their structural elements and organizing these elements according to certain mapping rules. In other words, the degree to which one perceives appropriately

	1	2	3	4	5
I	Given drawing of 5 pin geoboard with 2 rubber bands, trace pattern.			Given drawing of 25 pin geoboard with 10 rubber bands, draw pattern on 25 dot map.	Given drawing of 25 pin geoboard with 12 rubber bands, draw pattern on 0 dot map.
H			Given drawing of 25 pin geoboard with 8 rubber bands, construct pattern on 25 pin geoboard.	Given drawing of 25 pin geoboard with 8 rubber bands, draw pattern on 25 dot map.	Given drawing of 25 pin geoboard with 7 rubber bands, draw pattern on 9 dot map.
G			Given drawing of 25 pin geoboard with 5 rubber bands, construct pattern on 25 pin geoboard.	Given drawing of 25 pin geoboard with 5 rubber bands, draw pattern on 25 dot map.	Given drawing of 25 pin geoboard with 4 rubber bands, draw pattern on 17 dot map.
F			Given drawing of 25 pin geoboard with 3 rubber bands, construct pattern on 9 pin geoboard.	Given drawing of 25 pin geoboard with 3 rubber bands, draw pattern on 25 dot map.	
E			Given drawing of 9 pin geoboard with 3 rubber bands, construct pattern on 9 pin geoboard.	Given drawing of 9 pin geoboard with 3 rubber bands, draw pattern on 9 dot map.	
D		Given 5 pin geoboard with 2 rubber bands, duplicate pattern on 5 pin geoboard.	Given drawing of 5 pin geoboard with 2 rubber bands, construct pattern on 5 pin geoboard.	Given drawing of 5 pin geoboard with 2 rubber bands, draw pattern on 5 dot map.	
C	Given 5 pin geoboard with 2 rubber bands, superimpose rubber bands.	Given 5 pin geoboard with 3 rubber bands, duplicate pattern (model and test board are color coded).	Given drawing of 5 pin geoboard with 2 rubber bands, construct pattern on 5 pin geoboard (model and test board color coded).		
B	Given 2 direction cube arrangement, superimpose cubes.	Given 2 direction cube arrangement, duplicate model.	Given drawing of squares, duplicate pattern with cubes.		
A	Given 1 direction cube arrangement, superimpose cubes.	Given 1 direction cube arrangement, duplicate model.			

Figure 4-10

Behavioral objectives summary of Program I: Visual-Motor Skills

	1	2	3	4	5	6	7	8	9
H						Given 2 spoken words and designated medial sound, identify word that contains sound.	Given spoken word with a 2 consonant blend, then word with 1 sound omitted, identify omitted sound.	Given spoken word, repeat, omitting one sound of a 2 consonant blend.	Given spoken word, substitute any sound with another designated sound.
G						Given 2 spoken words and designated consonant sound, indicate which word ends with sound.	Given spoken word 1 syllable word, then word with final sound omitted, identify omitted sound.	Given spoken 1 syllable word, repeat, omitting final sound.	Given spoken 1 syllable word, substitute beginning or ending sound with another designated sound.
F						Given 2 spoken words and a designated sound, indicate which word begins with sound.	Given spoken word 1 syllable word, then word with initial sound omitted, identify omitted sound.	Given spoken 1 syllable word, repeat word omitting initial sound.	
E				Given spoken 3 or 4 syllable word, say and clap simultaneously with each syllable.	Given spoken 3 syllable word, "write" syllables with dashes and "read" dash requested.	Given spoken 3 syllable word, indicate presence or absence of specified syllable.	Given spoken 3 syllable word, then 2 of the syllables, say which syllable was omitted.	Given spoken 3 syllable word, repeat word, omitting designated syllable.	
D				Given spoken pair of 2 syllable words, say and clap simultaneously with each syllable.	Given spoken phrase of 1 and 2 syllable words, "write" syllable with dash and "read" dash requested.	Given spoken 2 syllable word, indicate presence or absence of specified syllable.	Given spoken 2 syllable word, then only one of the syllables, say omitted syllable.	Given spoken 2 word series, repeat, omitting 1 designated word.	
C				Given spoken phrase of 1 syllable words, "write" each word and clap simultaneously.	Given spoken phrase of 1 syllable words, "write" each word with dash and "read" dash requested.	Given spoken series of 1 syllable words, indicate presence or absence of specified word.	Given spoken series of 3 1 syllable words, then same series with 1 word omitted, say omitted word.		
B	Given music, changing tempo, clap in synchrony.	Given long and short claps, draw dashes in synchrony.	Given long and short claps, reproduce pattern.	Given spoken numerals, clap once for each.	Given spoken numerals, draw a dash for each numeral.				
A	Given march music, clap in synchrony.	Given series of claps, draw a dash for each.	Given series of claps, reproduce pattern.						

Figure 4-11

Behavioral objectives summary of Program II: Auditory-Motor Skills (in terms of school learning) is a function of his capacity to break spatial and semantic patterns into their component parts and recognize the interrelationships—spatial and temporal—of those parts. It follows that, having acquired this capacity, coding and de-coding those component parts, such as is required in classroom programs of reading, spelling, and arithmetic instruction, are more likely to make sense to the student. This will be evident in the relative ease with which the student acquires the concepts involved in relating phoneme to grapheme and recognizing that the temporal relationships of the phonemes are the equivalent of the spatial relationships of the graphemes; and in relating numerals to the quantity of elements in a spatial array, as well as recognizing that numerals can also function as the organizers of the Euclidean space that contains the spatial array.

Third, young children analyze and organize visual and acoustical patterns more effectively if they are able to explore the sensory stimuli in some tangible fashion.[19] The learning activities of the curriculum, designed to teach these analytical and organizational skills, reflect the assumptions stated above. The Visual-Motor program teaches the child how to reconstruct spatial patterns. The patterns are relatively simple at the lower levels, and the space where they are to be placed is clearly mapped. For example, simple geometric designs, drawn on a map of five dots, are copied with rubber bands onto a geoboard—a board containing an arrangement of nails that is identical to the map of dots. As the child makes progress, the geoboard is replaced with a second paper map of dots, and the patterns become a bit more complex. The designs become even more complex at a higher level, and more dots are included on the map. The dots are gradually eliminated from the map used at the highest levels, and the child learns to "imagine the dots are there." (Figure 4-12 shows representative tasks from the program at various levels of complexity.) Thus, as the child reaches this level, he demonstrates that he has learned both to analyze complex patterns and to organize the space in which they appear. Stated another way, he has learned to recognize both the absolute and the relational attributes of geometric designs. The value of this, in terms of school achievement, is evident. Learning to use numerals to code these attributes is a reasonable undertaking.

The Auditory program teaches the child to analyze spoken words

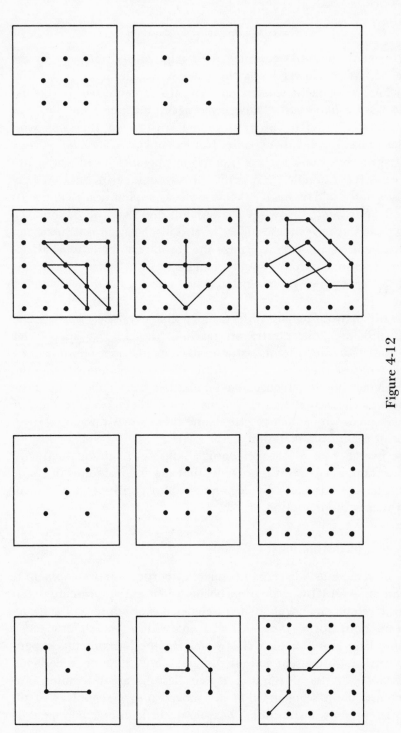

Figure 4-12

Representative tasks for Visual-Motor Program: Lower and higher levels (The child reproduces the left-hand pattern in the right-hand frame.)

into segments and to recognize their relative positions within the sequence. At the lower levels the student engages in activities that teach him to segment spoken phrases into separate words (for example "Say *I like you*"; "Now say it again, but don't say *you*"; or "Don't say *I*"). As he progresses he learns to do the same with smaller units: words into syllables (for example, "Say *picnic*"; "Now say it again, but don't say *pic*"; or "Don't say *nic*"); and words into phonemes (for example, "Say *gate*"; "Now say it again, but don't say the /g/ sound"; "Say *meat*"; "Now say it again, but don't say the /t/ sound"; "Say *slap*"; "Now say it again, but don't say the /s/ sound"). As the child achieves these higher level skills, he again is demonstrating that he has learned to recognize the absolute and relational attributes of a sensory pattern—spoken language in this instance. Learning to use letters to code these attributes will now be a reasonable undertaking.

The other two programs reflect similar characteristics. The General-Motor program concentrates on teaching the child to analyze his own body scheme into its structural elements and recognize the organization of those elements. The Letters and Numerals program, as the name implies, focuses on familiarizing the child with those symbols to the extent that he can distinguish them, point to them as they are named by someone else, name them when they are shown, and print them from dictation.

The overall goal of the Perceptual Skills Curriculum, then, is to make certain, insofar as it is possible, that the child acquires the basic perceptual skills assumed by beginning reading, arithmetic, and spelling programs of instruction.

Evaluation of Instructional Programs

An integral and indispensable aspect of curriculum development is evaluation. At LRDC evaluation begins when initial curriculum and lesson development begins. When new lessons are proposed and prepared in draft form, they are tried out with a few children, in a teaching laboratory or in a classroom. On the basis of this experience, curriculum content and instructional procedures are redesigned or discarded. After this initial tryout, lessons are assembled into larger curriculum segments that are moved into a school as an adjunct to present instruction. The new curriculum component is evaluated by teachers, students, and parents with respect to teach-ability, relevance to school population, instructional efficiency, school interest, and instructional effects. Following this, a revised version is moved into a classroom as the major instructional program in that subject matter. A revision based on this experience is then introduced into several classes. It is usually efficient with respect to available resources and effective school management to introduce a program into a classroom at one grade level each school year, carry-ing the students along through the program as they progress in school. This allows the developers to assess an ongoing program while they develop it further. Evaluation of the effects of the new program can be carried out at the same time, by making comparisons with classroom practices and student performance in the school year im-mediately prior to the introduction of the new program. This proce-dure avoids, at this point, the complexity of comparisons between groups from different schools.[20] Following evaluation in a develop-mental school, in which much observation and special assistance are required, the program is then disseminated to field test schools that provide a diversity of school populations and more realistic school environments. A new program is moved into the field only when the assessment of effects and the nature of implementation in the devel-opmental schools appear encouraging.

In the field schools a central problem arises concerning the differ-ent ways in which a particular instructional program is implemented in different classes; changes often occur as the program moves away from the artificial bolstering of the initial developmental situation. A procedure is needed for determining the ways in which, and the extent to which, each classroom or school actually implements the instructional program. These measures of the degree of implementa-tion of important classroom variables then need to be related to the performance of children. Because the evaluation of new programs is a complex problem, LRDC has worked not only on the evaluation of its particular programs, but, under the direction of William Cooley, has developed a general model for research on evaluation.[21]

With respect to cost, experience to date indicates that implementa-tion of individualized systems of the kind described in this chapter requires an increase in cost over conventional educational programs equivalent to the expense of having a teacher aide in the classroom. It has been found, however, that aides drawn from the local school community are increasingly being employed by schools both as a means of assisting in classrooms and of bringing individuals in the community closer to the schools that serve their children.

An adequate evaluation of educational innovations requires multivariate examination of the influence of, and relationship between, four domains of variables: characteristics of the student population; properties of the instructional model, including curriculum components, the teaching practices involved, and the classroom environment that results; characteristics of the school and the ways in which the new program is implemented; and assessment of the achievements of students, both planned and unintended.

A Look Ahead

As part of its work in curriculum development and instructional research LRDC has conducted a project to integrate computer assistance into an adaptive mode. The present work of the project at the Oakleaf School is concerned with three areas: investigation of the use of computers for instructional assistance, including testing, classroom data management, tutorial instruction, drill and practice, exploration and discovery, and problem solving; the design of a small computer time-sharing system that can be used for both operations and research and that can eventually lead to the development of specifications for a small computer system especially suited for elementary school use; and investigation of basic techniques underlying work in computer-assisted instruction, such as instructional strategies in problem solving and inquiry, the appropriate timing and distribution of use of computerized practice exercises in arithmetic, spelling, and language arts, and the decision-making characteristics of computer testing.

At the present time, computer terminals are part of the classroom environment for students at Oakleaf and are used like other classroom materials for purposes of practicing one's skills in arithmetic and spelling, for testing accompanied by immediate knowledge of results, and for using one's newly acquired skills in problem-solving contexts. A system of queries has been designed whereby teachers, school administrators, and researchers can obtain computer printouts of a student's progress and of students grouped according to various criteria.[22]

This chapter has contrasted two modes of education—selective and adaptive. One exists in present-day schools. The other we aspire to.[23] The currently prevalent mode of education is characterized by minimal variation in the conditions under which individuals are expected to learn. A relatively narrow range of instructional options is provided; a limited number of ways to succeed are available. The adaptability of the system to the student is, consequently, limited, and alternative paths that can be selected for students with different backgrounds and talents are restricted. In such an environment, the options that are available require that students have particular abilities, and these *particular* abilities are emphasized and fostered to the exclusion of other abilities.

In contrast to this relatively fixed selective mode of education, newer conceptions suggest a mere adaptive educational mode. An adaptive mode assumes that the educational environment can provide a range and variety of instructional methods and opportunities for success. Alternate means of learning are adaptive to and in some way matched to knowledge about each individual: his background, talents, interests, and the nature of his past performance. An individual's styles and abilities are assessed either upon entrance to or during the course of learning, and certain educational paths are elected or assigned. Further information is obtained about the learner as learning proceeds, and this information is, in turn, related to subsequent alternate learning opportunities. The interaction between performance and the subsequent nature of the educational setting is the defining characteristic of an adaptive mode, and the success of this adaptive interaction is determined by the extent to which the student experiences some kind of a match between his specific abilities and interests and the activities in which he engages. The effect of any instructional path would be evaluated by the changes it brings about in the student's potential for future learning and attainment of goals; measures of individual differences are valid to the extent that they help to define alternate paths that result in optimizing immediate learning as well as long-term success.

Notes

1. C. Mauritz Lindvall and John O. Belvin, "Programed Instruction in the Schools: An Application of Programing Principles in 'Individually Prescribed

Instruction,' " in *Programed Instruction*, ed. Phil C. Lange, Sixty-sixth Yearbook of the National Society for the Study of Education, Part II (Chicago: University of Chicago Press, 1967), 217-54.

2. Robert Glaser and L. B. Resnick, "Instructional Psychology," in *Annual Review of Psychology*, Vol. 23, ed. P. H. Mussen and M. R. Rosenzweig (Palo Alto: Annual Reviews, 1972), 207-76.

3. Robert Glaser, "Individuals and Learning: The New Aptitudes," *Educational Researcher* 1 (June 1972): 5-13.

4. Robert Glaser, "Evaluation of Instruction and Changing Educational Models," in *The Evaluation of Instruction*, ed. Merle C. Wittrock and David E. Wiley (New York: Holt, Rinehart and Winston, 1970), 70-86.

5. The following material has been excerpted from Robert Glaser, "Adapting the Elementary School Curriculum to Individual Performance," in *Proceedings of the 1967 Invitational Conference on Testing Problems* (Princeton, N.J.: Educational Testing Service, 1968), 3-36.

6. Edwin A. Fleishman, "The Description and Prediction of Perceptual-Motor Skill Learning," in *Training Research and Education*, ed. Robert Glaser (New York: John Wiley, 1965), 137-76.

7. The following material has been excerpted from I. L. Beck and D. D. Mitroff, *The Rationale and Design of a Primary Grades Reading System for an Individualized Classroom* (Pittsburgh: Learning Research and Development Center, University of Pittsburgh, 1972).

8. The following material has been excerpted from Leopold Klopfer, "Individualized Science: Relevance for the 1970's," *Science Education* 55 (October 1971): 441-48; and from Audrey B. Champagne, "A Realistic Approach for Developing Science Inquiry Skills," a paper presented at the meeting of the National Science Teachers Association, Washington, D.C., March 1971.

9. Klopfer, *op. cit.*, 447.

10. *Ibid.*

11. The following material has been excerpted from L. B. Resnick, M. C. Wang, and Jerome Rosner, "Adaptive Education for Young Children: The Primary Education Project," in *The Preschool in Action*, ed. R. K. Parker (Boston: Allyn and Bacon, in press).

12. J. H. Flavell, "Stage-Related Properties of Cognitive Development," *Cognitive Psychology* 2 (October 1971): 421-543; Sheldon H. White, "Evidence for a Hierarchical Arrangement of Learning Processes," in *Advances in Child Development and Behavior*, Vol. 2, ed. Lewis P. Lipsitt and Charles C. Spiker (New York: Academic Press, 1965), 187-220.

13. Robert M. Gagné, "Contributions of Learning to Human Development," *Psychological Review* 75 (May 1968): 177-91.

14. Lawrence Kohlberg, "Early Education: A Cognitive Developmental View," *Child Development* 39 (December 1968): 1013-62.

15. J. McVicker Hunt, *The Challenge of Incompetence and Poverty* (Urbana: University of Illinois Press, 1969).

16. L. B. Resnick, *Design of an Early Learning Curriculum* (Pittsburgh: Learning Research and Development Center, University of Pittsburgh, 1967).

17. Robert Glaser, "A Criterion-Referenced Test," in *Criterion-Referenced Measurement: An Introduction*, ed. W. J. Popham (Englewood Cliffs, N.J.: Educational Technology Publications, 1971), 41-51.

18. Jerome Rosner, *The Development and Validation of an Individualized Perceptual Skills Curriculum* (Pittsburgh: Learning Research and Development Center, University of Pittsburgh, 1972).

19. Jean Piaget, *Psychology of Intelligence* (Paterson, N.J.: Littlefield, Adams and Co., 1960); J. S. Bruner *et al.*, *Studies in Cognitive Growth* (New York: John Wiley, 1967).

20. William W. Cooley, *Methods of Evaluating School Innovations* (Pittsburgh: Learning Research and Development Center, University of Pittsburgh, 1971).

21. *Ibid.*

22. Reports of this work are presented in William W. Cooley and Robert Glaser, "The Computer and Individualized Instruction," *Science* 166 (October 1969): 574-82; Robert Glaser and William W. Cooley, "Instrumentation for Teaching and Instructional Management," in *Second Handbook of Research on Teaching*, ed. Robert M. W. Travers (Chicago: Rand McNally, 1973), 207-76; K. K. Block *et al.*, *A Computer Resource for the Elementary School: Progress Report 1971-1972* (Pittsburgh: Learning Research and Development Center, University of Pittsburgh, 1973); R. L. Ferguson, *Computer Assistance for Individualizing Measurement* (Pittsburgh: Learning Research and Development Center, University of Pittsburgh, 1971); T. Hsu and M. Carlson, *Computer-Assisted Achievement Testing* (Pittsburgh: Learning Research and Development Center, University of Pittsburgh, 1971); and R. J. Fitzhugh, "Computer-Assisted Instructional System: Computer Requirements," a paper presented at a meeting of the American Psychological Association, Montreal, Canada, August 1973.

23. Glaser, "Individuals and Learning: The New Aptitudes."

5. An Individualized Instructional System: PLAN*

John C. Flanagan, William M. Shanner,
Harvey J. Brudner, and *Robert W. Marker*

Introduction

PLAN* (Program for Learning in Accordance with Needs) is an individualized multimedia system of education built upon a data base of instructional objectives, learning resources, performance tests, and personalized programs of study in reading and language arts, mathematics, science, and social studies. The system continues in development and is being marketed by Westinghouse Learning Corporation.[1] It is adaptive to a wide variety of school facilities and budgets.

The basic building block in PLAN* is the TLU ("Teaching-Learning Unit"), which includes instructional objectives associated with recommended learning activities and criterion tests. A guidance system uses data on students and draws upon a bank of available TLU's to recommend an individualized program of studies (POS) for each student. The POS is individualized on the basis of both the number and type of activities the student pursues.

A computer facility is used in PLAN* to collect information concerning the progress and performance of students from terminals located in the participating schools. This information is processed for feedback to students and teachers and is stored for record-keeping purposes and for use in the management aspects of the system.

A correlated training program for administrators and teachers assists both in developing the techniques necessary to implement the individualized education system. PLAN* utilizes, by this means, the school's existing administrative and instructional staff in performing the functions of counseling and classroom management required by the system.

Origin of the System

The immediate stimulus for the development of the PLAN* educational system was the Project TALENT Survey of 1960.[2] This survey, financed by the U.S. Office of Education and conducted by the American Institutes for Research (AIR), included a two-day battery of tests and questionnaires and was given to about 440,000 students in the ninth through the twelfth grades of a stratified random sample of secondary schools of all types throughout the United States. Some of the more striking findings of this study concerned the very large individual differences in the level of ability and amount of knowledge among the students in any one of the grades. It was found, for example, that between 25 percent and 30 percent of ninth-grade students had already achieved as much knowledge and ability in such fields as English and social studies as the average twelfth-grade student. This great variability in the level of achievement of the students in a particular class suggested a real need for individualization of the educational program.

A second finding from Project TALENT, pointing to the need for both individualization and curriculum change, related to the appraisals of the students regarding their opportunities for learning. In the survey in 1960, 49 percent of the students indicated that "about half the time or more frequently lack of interest in my school work makes it difficult for me to keep my attention on what I am doing." Similarly, 28 percent of the students reported that "most of the time, or almost always, I feel that I am taking courses that will not help me much in an occupation after I leave school." In an update of this survey conducted in a sample of the schools in March 1970[3] the students were asked the question, "In relation to what you could have learned with the best learning methods and materials, how much did you learn during the past year?" About 43 percent of both boys and girls indicated that they had learned 10 percent to 50 percent of what they could have learned. Only about 12 percent of both the boys and the girls thought they had learned 90 percent of what they could have learned. In answer to the question, "How well do your school courses meet your needs?" about 51 percent of the boys and 61 percent of the girls reported "well" or "very well," while 18 percent of the boys and 11 percent of the girls reported "a little" or "not at all."

Both of these findings point to the need for developing a truly individualized educational program for each child. Such a program would include not only the type of individualized instruction that has long been regarded as essential for effective education, but also an individualized set of educational objectives for each child.

For this type of educational program to be functional, the individual student must take the responsibility for formulating goals, making decisions and plans with respect to his educational development, and managing the learning program required to achieve the goals he has set.

In addition to these findings from the Project TALENT surveys, a number of trends and conditions provided a setting for designing an effective educational system at the present time. The most obvious trend in American education is the change from a system for educating the elite to one for educating all children. In the last sixty years there has been a dramatic change in the proportion of those entering the first grade who go on to complete high school (10 percent in 1910 and 70 percent in 1970).

A second trend of great importance for education is the enormous expansion of available knowledge. The number of books in print is increasing exponentially, and instead of a fixed set of basic skills and a defined amount of academic knowledge to be learned, educators are faced with a program of assisting students to select the skills, abilities, appreciations, and knowledge likely to be most valuable in achieving their goals. It is fortunate that the changes concerning a widely varied group of students and a greatly expanded set of possible learning experiences have been accompanied by a third major change: the rapid increase in technology. It is essential that education make full use of technological advances including audio and visual equipment. In addition to classroom-controlled items, radio, television, and electronic computers are needed to assist with the increased complexity of the educational program.

Strategies and Approaches for Improving Education

That the foregoing problems and deficiencies in education could be solved in a traditional educational framework was improbable for several reasons. First, the existing structure of education did not provide adequately for a wide range of individual differences and the resulting variability in achievement characteristic of any age or grade group. Second, schools generally neglected to develop in students a sense of responsibility that they need in order to make decisions concerning their education and career. Third, the usual objectives of education failed fully to prepare students for productive occupations, responsible citizenship, or satisfying adulthood. And fourth, current teaching methods lacked the effectiveness, efficiency, and flexibility to reach levels of skill, understanding, and competence known to be attainable.

The development of an educational system that could overcome these deficiencies necessarily had to be concerned with a number of practical realities. The technology had to be within the budget capabilities of most school districts, and any changes required by the system had to be operationally feasible. It also was recognized that present knowledge about individual differences, the learning process, teaching aids and materials, curriculum design, the management of educational resources, and other likely components of an optimal system is far from complete. To wait for detailed solutions to all expected problems, on the other hand, would cause needless delays in the application of all that was known. For this reason, an approach was devised that permitted continuous improvements in the system after its introduction. No changes in physical space, classroom personnel, or administrative responsibilities were contemplated, and a decision was made to limit the selection of instructional materials to what was commercially available. Significant steps were planned, however, in the establishment of educational objectives, the organization of instructional sequences, the use of evaluative data, and the way in which a typical classroom would operate.

The development of PLAN* was not based on any one particular learning or instructional theory. It was founded, rather, on the belief that an educational program should use the individual student and his needs as the basis for a complete educational system. Each student should actively participate in planning his educational program and should take some responsibility for managing both the strategy and tactics for achieving his goal by using learning materials and engaging in learning activities that suited his abilities and interests. His progress should be continually monitored and rewarded. PLAN* is, in short, based on the philosophy of individual planning, individualized instruction, and continuous evaluation.

The general approach adopted for PLAN*s developmental effort involved four principal strategies.

The first strategy was to focus the system on the appropriate development of each individual student. This approach immediately places the student where he should be—at the center of the program —while teachers, school buildings, textbooks, media, technology, and all other aspects of the educational program are cast in supporting and subordinate roles. At the same time this approach necessarily gives prime importance to outcomes. It requires the appraisal of each student as an input to the educational system and the determination of the specific types of development most appropriate to his leaving that system with the ability, skill, knowledge, and appreciation that will assist him in obtaining the quality of life he has planned. Such a strategy immediately places great emphasis on determining the relevance for each individual of various types of educational development and requires that both his long-term and short-term objectives be clearly stated and that suitable procedures be developed for assessing the achievement of each objective.

The second strategy was to make a comprehensive and systematic study of all the resources available for assisting students to achieve this development. This important aspect of the developmental effort requires that available learning methods and materials be carefully reviewed in terms of the specific objectives of various types of students. It further requires that possible aid from technological resources be studied and that new roles and procedures for teachers and other educational personnel be reviewed in terms of the efficiency and effectiveness of various approaches. Improvements cannot be anticipated unless this design phase is comprehensive and insightful.

The third strategy was to place the responsibility for developing the educational system in the hands of a balanced team of qualified specialists. To design an efficient educational program to meet the needs of all students, the experience and judgment of classroom teachers regarding the interests and learning habits of students should be fully utilized. Their experience should be especially helpful in identifying the learning methods and materials to be used by specific types of students for achieving specific objectives. The aid of curriculum experts and scholars from various disciplines is essential in deciding on both the content and objectives most appropriate for preparing specific types of students for long-range goals. School administrators must assist in the design and adaptation of this type of educational approach to ensure that the system meets local needs and problems. Finally, the design and development staff must include behavioral scientists with experience in both classroom activities and educational technology to make certain that the findings and procedures of research and development in education and related fields are fully utilized.

The fourth strategy was to utilize a management information system to make complete information on each student's progress available to all those involved in both the developmental and operational phases of the program. This is an obvious but often neglected aspect of the development of a system. Accountability in education is becoming increasingly important for school administrators. It is no longer sufficient to provide those supporting the schools such information as the number of the students, the number of teachers, the number of class hours of instruction, and their relative costs. Both parents and taxpayers are demanding to know what increases in student competence and preparation for life accompany growing school costs. An important source of motivation for both students and teachers is knowledge of the progress attained with respect to important objectives. Assurance of continued improvement in the functioning of a system cannot possibly be obtained without a comprehensive program of evaluating student learning in relation to specific procedures and programs.

**Basic Functions to Be Performed
by an Individualized Educational System**

An individualized educational system must include many elements and functions. Many of them are either secondary or perhaps even incidental to the basic functions that concern only the development of the individual. There are, however, three basic functions.

To assist each individual to formulate specific goals for his individual educational development is the first basic function. It is usually thought of in terms of a program of guidance and counseling to aid the student in making decisions concerning his education, career, citizenship, and personal development. This program is complex and ambitious because of the need to assist young people in making their own choices and decisions from among the increasing number of alternatives now available.

The second basic function, to aid each student to identify and participate in learning experiences that will enable him to achieve his educational goals, is, of course, central to any educational system. It involves many factors such as learning methods and materials, the role of the teacher, and the use of audiovisual materials and other technological aids.

To evaluate the progress of each student toward achieving his goals constitutes the third basic function and is essential if the procedures described in the first two functions are performed less than perfectly. Such an evaluation provides the data to be used by the student in reevaluating his goals in terms of his experience in trying to achieve them. It supplies the basic data to evaluate the effectiveness of the learning experiences, and it makes possible effective management of the system. By accumulating information regarding the types of methods and materials that best suit a student, it furnishes a basis for selecting future learning experiences.

Development of the PLAN* Educational System

The need for a new approach to educational problems became clear in 1961 when the findings from the Project TALENT Survey were analyzed. However, although the presentation and publication of papers and reports did seem to have some impact on educational programs, the effects were relatively small and somewhat isolated. It gradually became clear that only through development and demonstration could the basic implications of the findings of Project TALENT be adequately utilized in American educational programs. After AIR made some abortive attempts to obtain support for setting up a small experimental school, it was found that a number of school administrators were interested in cooperating in the development of such a program. At about this same time, during 1966, plans were being made by Westinghouse Electric Company to create a major new educational subsidiary. In January 1967 an agreement was signed by the American Institutes for Research in the Behavioral Sciences, the Westinghouse Learning Corporation, and fourteen cooperating school systems.[4]

The school districts, covering large cities, suburbs, and rural areas, provided teachers and staff members at the expense of the school districts to develop the instructional components of the program, as well as the teachers, classrooms, and students with which PLAN* was experimentally operated during its developmental period from 1967 to 1971. The developmental activities were under the combined administrative supervision of the American Institutes for Research and the Research and Development Group of Westinghouse Learning Corporation. Westinghouse Learning Corporation provided the major funding for the initial development of PLAN*, implemented the program as it developed, and now has complete responsibility for development and dissemination of PLAN*.[5]

The schedule called for the development of the PLAN* educational system for the first through the twelfth grades in the areas of reading and language arts, mathematics, science, social studies, and guidance over a four-year period, 1967-1971. From February 1967 through August of that year the program was developed for the first, fifth, and ninth grades, with a tryout of the program in two classrooms (sixty students) in each of twelve schools (total of about 700 students per grade) at each of the three grade levels during the school year 1967-1968. The next cycle called for the development of the instructional program for the second, sixth, and tenth grades from September 1967 through August 1968, with the tryout in the schools during the following year. The third cycle provided for the development and tryout for the third, seventh, and eleventh grades, and the final cycle in the fourth year for the development and tryout for the fourth, eighth, and twelfth grades. Thus, over the four cycles, a continuous learning sequence for the first through the twelfth grades in the areas of reading and language arts, mathematics, science, social studies, and guidance was developed, tried out, and revised. Fourteen school districts comprising some 8,000 cooperating students and 280 teachers, together with eighty professional staff members of the American Institutes for Research, were involved in the developmental activities of PLAN*. An extensive technical, clerical, and secretarial staff was also required.

A bibliography[6] citing seventy-one titles of published articles, reports, and presentations given at meetings of professional organizations describes various developmental activities of PLAN* during the period 1967-1970.

The behaviorally stated instructional objectives and learning activities were developed by experienced classroom teachers provided by the cooperating school districts, each of which sent one teacher per year for every level being developed to the office of the American Institutes for Research in Palo Alto. In the first cycle (February-August 1967) there were twelve teachers each for the first, fifth, and ninth grades, or a total of thirty-six teachers. These teachers returned the following year to their schools to try out the programs that they had developed. The schools sent new teams of teachers at the various levels to AIR's office in Palo Alto for each of the following three cycles. Working with these teachers was a team including experienced school administrators, subject-matter specialists, and behavioral scientists with special expertise in measurement and evaluation and educational psychology. To supplement this group, particularly with respect to decisions regarding curriculum and general objectives, the services of sixteen distinguished leaders in language arts, social science, science, and mathematics were obtained. These people served as both individual consultants and panelists on four national curriculum advisory panels.

In developing the system, many products and activities had to be completed. The principal ones are described briefly below:

1. Educational objectives. Rather than carry on extensive new studies to develop a comprehensive list of objectives in language arts, social studies, science, and mathematics for the first through the twelfth grades, it was decided to utilize recently published reports of various curriculum groups. Outlines of the general scope and content in each of the fields for the twelve levels were developed, with the assistance of the advisory panels.

The experienced teachers from the cooperating schools then used these outlines to identify positive learning activities and effective instructional activities in each area for each level. The learning activities were then stated in behavioral terms that expressed what the student was expected to do (for example, multiply any three-digit number by any three-digit number) when the objective was mastered. The objectives were organized into a curriculum for the subject area at that level, but no single rigid plan or sequence was established. There was, rather, a sampling of selected modern curriculum studies and courses or programs of typical school systems. Thus, PLAN* was not restricted to one particular philosophy of education or system of values; it was developed as an operating program rather than a directional one. The curriculum at each level was checked for omissions against various standard courses of study, including local and state requirements of the cooperating schools, for overlap with other levels, and for relevance to current educational needs. The total set of objectives was much more extensive than any single student could master in his educational career. By selecting subsets of the objectives, schools were able to adapt the curriculum and meet local conditions and requirements. Then, within the curriculum for each school, a unique subset of objectives (program of studies) could be selected to individualize the program for each student. The original set of approximately 6,000 objectives are available in published form.[7]

2. Learning methods and materials. A basic initial decision was that the PLAN* educational system would utilize available instructional materials and media since many new educational programs have been developed with federal support during the past decade. There is, unfortunately, a serious lack of evaluative data regarding the effectiveness of these programs. It seemed desirable, nonetheless, rather than attempting to develop costly new programs, to select the more promising from among the available programs and materials and evaluate their effectiveness as one function of the system's developmental program.

The teachers from the cooperating schools reviewed the most promising and widely used instructional materials that were available. Following this, Teaching-Learning Units (TLU's) were developed for each instructional objective in the PLAN* system. Each TLU started with the objective that tells the student what he is going to learn. Then come steps of various learning activities that specify the instructional materials to use and the activities to do. These learning activities are designed to help the student master the objective. A TLU contains no learning materials per se; it is a guide to the use of these materials. A wide range of learning activities was selected for inclusion in the TLU's. It is important at this point to clarify some misconceptions. Individualized instruction is not the same as independent study or learning in isolation. To be sure, independent study is often a part of individualized instruction, but so are the other typical learning activities found in the classroom including discussion groups, working in pairs, small-group instruction, large-group instruction, and the like. Individualized instruction is a larger idea using a variety of techniques, procedures, and materials to accomplish the learning needs of individual students. Alternate TLU's were developed for many objectives where different sets of instructional materials and learning activities are referenced to the same objectives. In this connection it is recognized that there are many ways or many such instructional materials involving many different types of learning activities that will lead to accomplishment of the same objective. Alternate TLU's provide students with a choice of ways to master an objective. Such a choice permits various programs of studies to be adapted to individual differences.

At the conclusion of the program, some 12,000 different instructional items (textbooks, filmstrips, workbooks, games, and so forth) had been referenced to provide learning activities for the more than 6,000 instructional objectives developed for PLAN*. As new materials become available, it is only necessary to prepare TLU's utilizing these new resources in order to incorporate them into the PLAN* system.

3. Evaluation. The evaluation of both the progress of the student and the effectiveness of the materials is accomplished by criterion-referenced test exercises based upon every instructional objective. The tests focus on the mastery of the objectives. The student takes the test when he thinks he has mastered the objectives in TLU's; it determines whether he should go on to the next unit or study the materials of the present unit further. He is also tested for retention over a sequence of TLU's by an achievement test designed to measure the objectives covered by several TLU's or a segment of the curriculum. This same test, if administered to a new student or to a student prior to his studying that segment of the curriculum, performs a placement function by identifying the objectives in the segment that he has not mastered. Used in this manner, it helps establish individualized programs of studies for each student. Hence, the tests covering several TLU's are called Placement/Achievement Tests.

4. Guidance and individual planning. As indicated previously, assisting the student to formulate goals and plans is one of the basic

functions of the PLAN* educational system. Since satisfactory
materials were not available in this area, a major effort was made to
produce materials that could be used to accomplish this function.
The five parts of this program were developed to achieve the following:

a. To acquaint the student with the varieties of opportunities,
roles, and activities available in the fields of occupations,
personal, social, and civic relations, and in cultural, recreational,
and other leisure-time pursuits. This information includes the
educational requirements for specific careers and the levels of
achievement in terms of developed abilities required for
entrance and effective work in these occupations. Information
on the importance of each of the roles and special conditions
relating to it is also provided.

b. To acquaint the student with the status of his development with
respect to abilities, interests, physical and social characteristics,
and values in the areas of education, occupations, citizenship,
and the use of leisure time. It is believed essential that as a part
of this program the student learn the nature of individual differences and the basic principles underlying learning activities.

c. To assist each student to formulate his long-term goals and to
take the responsibility for and plan a developmental program to
achieve these goals. This includes assisting the student to relate
his personal potentials for developing specific abilities, interests,
and values to the various opportunities likely to be available to
him. Included here is specific training in decision making and
problem solving.

d. To assist the student to acquire competence in managing his
own development. To the greatest extent possible, it is proposed to assist students in learning to carry out a program of
personal reinforcement of desirable behaviors in order to
correct and improve their behavioral patterns.

e. To assist the student in making a smooth transition from high
school to the world of work, higher education, and civic responsibilities.

5. *Teacher development.* It is believed essential that each new
teacher be prepared for the new role required by the PLAN* educational system. To keep this as efficient as possible, a four-phase
program was set up during the developmental phase of PLAN*. The

first is an orientation phase in which the teacher visits PLAN* classes being conducted by experienced teachers and participates in a program of directed observation and orientation. The orientation phase is usually conducted in the spring of the year prior to teachers' participation in the PLAN* system. The observation period is followed by the second phase, an informal reading period extending over the summer. The reading materials include discussions of the basic concepts and philosophy underlying PLAN* and individualized education in general. The third phase, usually conducted in late August, consists of a three- or four-day individualized program that uses modules, TLU's, objectives, and tests designed to acquaint the teacher with the basic information and skills essential for conducting a class in the PLAN* system. The last phase is an in-service training program. An appropriate supervisor observes the teacher at intervals during the early days of application of PLAN* and checks mastery on specific skills important to the effective functioning of PLAN* in the classroom.

As an important part of the total project, the twelve teachers who worked at AIR in Palo Alto on the development of the program in a particular grade used the system in their schools during the following academic year. In each of these schools an additional teacher was given the brief training program just mentioned and also used the PLAN* system. Thus, about 700 students in a dozen school districts were involved in the tryout of each year's new materials.

As an integral part of the PLAN* system, the computer monitored the progress of each child and reported the results back to the students and teachers. The teachers also noted specific difficulties with the learning materials and methods selected for the student in a specific TLU and made suggestions for improving these learning programs. The items measuring mastery of each of the objectives were also analyzed by the computer, and those showing unexpected or unusual results were examined for ambiguities or other defects. On the basis of these results, errors or specific defects were corrected immediately in all the schools.

The principal use of the results, however, was a systematic revision of the TLU's and tests based on the results from this initial tryout year. During this period there was also considerable observation of teachers and students in the experimental classrooms for the purpose of making various types of improvements in the total system. A special function of this observation was to provide the basis for improving the teacher development program, including procedures for tutoring, classroom organization, and other classroom management procedures. Portions of the teacher development program were supported under a Title III contract (68-05331) with the U.S. Office of Education.

The PLAN* System in Operation

Although PLAN* is a structured system with instructional objectives, TLU's criterion tests, and a computer-based management and information system, it is not a mechanical system. One cannot put PLAN* in a classroom and have it run by itself. PLAN* requires the support and cooperative efforts of teachers, administrators, and students. It gives teachers and administrators the tools and resources necessary to individualize learning and make it a more successful experience for students; among these tools are developmentally sequenced objectives; suggested learning activities for each objective, enriched with tapes and filmstrips; criterion-referenced tests and detailed suggestions for teaching each objective in an individualized setting; placement tests to help students get started at the right place in each subject area; and a computer support system that helps teachers with record keeping and daily planning. All these components add up to a complete system of individualized instruction that permits each child to move ahead at his own pace and take more responsibility for his own learning.

Accordingly, considerable care and attention are given to installing PLAN* in a new school. To help administrators and teachers make the best use of PLAN* by adapting it to their own school and community, workshops are provided for them prior to the introduction of PLAN* into their schools.

The Administrator

Before going into PLAN*, administrators normally participate in ten days of intensive training. During the first week the emphasis is on the way to organize a school building and a teaching staff for a completely individualized program. Starting with a floor plan and a list of teachers and paraprofessional staff, each administrator decides how to make the best use of his physical facilities and available personnel. All the various possibilities of grouping, team teaching, and differentiated staffing are examined.

Since every school situation is different, PLAN* consultants work individually with each administrator to set up an organization that allows the most flexibility in meeting students' needs. Once a building and staff organization has been worked out, administrators are instructed in the use of the PLAN* computerized materials ordering system so that they might order support materials for their schools.

The second week of the training period concentrates on the role of administrators in working with teachers to bring about change and professional growth. Administrators are prepared to take major responsibility for both the preservice PLAN* teacher training program and for in-service work with teachers in the classroom after school has started. This involves becoming completely familiar with all PLAN* teacher workshop materials and making detailed plans for a preservice training conference.

In addition, much time is spent in helping administrators to identify the problems that arise in an individualized classroom. The use of videotapes and role playing enables administrators to learn techniques for solving problems and provides an opportunity to practice them. During training and throughout the school year, PLAN* consultants work closely with administrators to make sure that they have the knowledge they need to implement the program.

A 131-page technical handbook, *The PLAN* Administrator's Manual*, summarizes the workshop training and serves as a guide to the administrator for his role in PLAN*. The manual suggests ways and provides forms for observing teachers and students in classrooms where individualized instruction is going on.

Development of procedures for classroom observation was considered necessary since the activities of teachers and students differ greatly in individualized instruction as compared with typical group instruction. Techniques for analyzing student involvement, a form for recording and analyzing interruption by students, and student questionnaire forms are also included and discussed to assist the administrator in implementing PLAN* and making the environment in the classroom conducive to individualized instruction. It is believed that the success or failure of the PLAN* program in a school rests to a large extent in the hands of the building administrator.

The Teacher

The only requirement for PLAN* teachers is regular teacher certification. They should, however, be flexible enough to adapt individualizing techniques and tutoring skills to their usual teaching style. Teachers who have never used PLAN* normally receive up to five days of training by local school personnel prior to the opening of school in the fall.

Workshops for teachers are designed to simulate PLAN* classrooms. While they are learning about PLAN*, teachers get the experience of actually working in an individualized setting similar to the one they will develop and manage for the students in their own classrooms.

Teachers begin with room arrangement and materials organization for individualized classrooms. They study the PLAN* curriculum and learn to use orientation and placement materials to help students get started in the program. Each teacher acquires a thorough understanding of the PLAN* computer support system and how to use it to monitor progress of students. Emphasis is also placed on management of the classroom in an individualized setting.

All this information is presented to teachers in the form of objectives and TLU's, and there is a test for each objective. Workshop leaders assume the role of a PLAN* teacher in the classroom, answering questions, calling group discussions, and giving special help to those who need it.

Slides, filmstrips, audiotapes, and videotapes help bring ideas to life. By the end of the workshop, teachers are prepared to use PLAN* in their own classrooms—from the day school begins. A 104-page technical publication, *The PLAN* Teacher's Manual*, summarizes the workshop training and serves as a resource for the teacher throughout the year.

The role of the teacher changes in a program of individualized instruction from the role of a teacher in a typical group instruction program. By utilizing the computer for record keeping and management activities, the teacher is freed from many noninstructional functions and, accordingly, has more time to relate personally to youngsters in an instructional way. Thus, the teacher's main task in the classroom is to facilitate learning. It might be pointed out that students actually do not learn from teachers; they learn from materials in much the same way that sick people do not get well from doctors, but rather from medication. The doctor, however, is important in prescribing and facilitating the proper kind of medication, the same as the teacher is important in facilitating learning through the proper utilization of instructional materials in the classroom. This program, then, is designed to maximize the amount of time that a teacher is capable of working with youngsters who have problems in learning in order to facilitate that learning.

The computer also has an important role in PLAN*, but that role is vastly different from the role of the teacher. In no instance in PLAN* does the computer assume a teaching role. Its function is to monitor and operate an informational system that is used as backup support so that the teacher can maximize the amount of time spent relating directly to the students and helping them with learning problems.

The Student

Each PLAN* student has an individualized program of studies (POS) stored for him in the computer. The POS is a list of the objectives in each subject area that the student is expected to master in the next several weeks or months. In its reports the computer prints the POS for the student. The student, either by himself or with the aid of the teacher, selects and plans the specific objectives in the various subject areas in which he is working. This plan, which becomes the student's assignments or instructional program for the next few days, is filed with the computer to indicate the objectives on which the student is actively working and the date on which he starts. It is available and can be recalled by the teacher should she wish to confer with a student. And it is included as a regular part of daily reports to advise the teacher of the active assignments of each student.

The student then secures the TLU's for these active objectives and follows the prescribed learning activities for mastery of the objectives. There are a number of components within the TLU, some of which are related directly to the student and some to the teacher.

For the student a teaching-learning unit is developed for each objective. These TLU's tell the child what he is going to learn. The objectives are followed by various learning activities which are numbered sequentially as steps. Each step specifies the instructional support materials to use (textbook or reference material, pages to study, problems to work, experiments to perform, and so forth) and the activities to do. These learning activities work together to help the student master the objective.

The second component for the student is the activity sheet. A TLU may have from zero to two activity sheets. These sheets help students learn by providing practice in skills, solving problems, and so forth; they supplement the exercises cited in the instructional support materials. Students may be assigned a varying number of sheets, depending upon the amount of practice the particular student needs in order to learn.

The third component, an instructional guide, may or may not be a part of a TLU. These guides provide additional or missing information that is not supplied by the instructional support materials; they may be in the form of a page of explanation or description, a story that teaches a point, an example to make things clearer—almost anything, in fact, that leads to mastery of the objective. Instructional guides help make it possible for students to learn without constantly depending on the teacher.

Tests constitute the fourth component. For every TLU, teachers are provided with a way by which they can determine when a student has mastered the objective. Many are multiple-choice tests. Students mark their answers on cards, the cards are submitted to the computer for scoring, and results of the tests are given the following morning. This system frees teachers from much test scoring and record keeping. Some objectives do not, of course, lend themselves to computer-scored testing and need to be evaluated by the teacher. Criteria for teachers to use in their evaluations are provided in the Teacher Directions for such objectives. In these cases, the last step of the TLU will direct the student to perform a specific task and submit his completed work to the teacher. The results of teacher-evaluated tests are given to the computer and become part of the student's record.

The primary component of the TLU's for the use of the teacher are Teacher Directions, which provide complete information for every TLU in the PLAN* system. All instructional materials called for in the TLU are listed for easy reference. Suggestions are given for introducing the TLU and for helping students understand the objective. Any steps where the teacher must meet with students for a check or a group discussion are explained in detail.

Teacher Directions also give teachers information about how to evaluate the objective. In most cases there is a computer-scored test which saves the teacher the time of scoring the test and keeping records up to date. If the objective needs to be evaluated by the teacher, specific criteria for judging the student's learning are given in the Teacher Directions. They also contain answers to activity sheets and tests.

Most of the learning is paced and scheduled by the student himself. Because he knows exactly what objectives are to be achieved, he can spend as much or as little time as necessary on each one. He is free to use reference materials to pursue topics of immediate interest, to review difficult segments as often as he wishes, and to ask the teacher for assistance whenever he feels he needs help. Because he typically is assigned three or four TLU's in different subject-matter areas to work on simultaneously, he can distribute his efforts on any one day among several topics or concentrate on just one. By sharing in the responsibility for planning his school day, the student receives practice in making decisions relevant to his own career and educational development. And, by pacing his own instruction, the student has an opportunity to progress in accordance with his individual talents and needs.

When the student reaches the end of a TLU, he is given the test for that unit. The test is scored, and, on the basis of the student's performance relative to each objective, a summary recommendation is prepared. If the student learned all that was expected of him, he is informed that his work on that TLU is complete. If he missed some items relating to particular objectives, he may be asked to review certain segments of the instructional material either from the TLU he already used or, possibly, from another TLU which may cover the missed content from a slightly different perspective. In those occasional instances when the student has done poorly on the entire test, a conference between the student and the teacher takes place to identify the difficulty. It may be that the student was ill prepared for the particular module or that he selected a TLU that was ineffective for him. Appropriate remedial action will be planned by the teacher and the student together. This may include a restructuring of the student's POS or, possibly, just a redoing of the unit. When desirable, an alternate version of the test can be used to assess mastery following additional study.

In summary, the student's typical learning cycle is as follows: the student's POS is recalled from the computer; the student, with the teacher's help, selects TLU's on which he will work, and he sets the schedule for completion; the student interacts with various learning materials and with resource personnel; the student takes a test; the computer scores the test and adds data to the student's file; if the TLU is mastered, the teacher and the student confer on the next portion of the POS to be assigned; if the TLU is not mastered, the student is recycled with additional learning activities until he achieves mastery. As is evident from the foregoing description of the student's learning cycle in PLAN*, the system emphasizes active learning on the part of each student and attempts to develop him as an independent learner. In fact, one ninth grader described PLAN* by saying, "Oh, yes, I see you're putting the responsibility for learning back on the student." As a student becomes an independent learner, the importance of instructional materials increases because the student learns through the activities provided by these materials.

PLAN* is, then, directed toward the long-range educational goal of developing independent learners or teaching youngsters how to learn by themselves. Part of this involves developing the skills and ability in the student to make realistic choices and plans. Students are asked to make choices (within limits) about the activities in which they engage and to set goals (in terms of objectives and TLU's) for both the next few months and the current school year. As they advance into higher grades, students set goals and make plans of a long-range nature about their educational careers.

The PLAN* Curriculum

The total set of objectives and TLU's in PLAN* represents the instructional potential of the PLAN* curriculum. Local/schools can select from this total set to establish their own curriculum. This selection may depend, in large part, upon the amount and quantity of instructional support materials that the school wishes to use. Further, the PLAN* curriculum is not a closed system. If a school has developed local objectives, they can be meshed with the objectives selected from PLAN*, and the computer-management system will keep track of them. Further evidence of the flexibility of the PLAN* curriculum with computer management is that "individualized independent learning activities" can be added to an individual student's program of study. Examples of such activities are special reports and term projects.

Since a single school unit, a building and its instructional staff, usually does not have a range of students from kindergarten through grade twelve and beyond, the PLAN* curriculum has been organized into levels that reflect their use in the schools.

Levels 1-8

The most extensive use of PLAN* is in the first through the eighth grades. *The PLAN* Curriculum Overview* is a 350-page manual designed for teachers directing PLAN* in this grade range. It lists all the objectives in the system by subject area and level and gives teachers detailed suggestions for designing programs of study to fit the specific needs of each child. Recommended sequences and prerequisites are given, along with ideas for grouping objectives by content area. Placement and orientation procedures are also covered.

At this grade range, PLAN* offers five basic reading programs: Chandler, Miami, Sullivan, Ginn 360 Series, and Harper-Row Linguistic. Some schools use only one program; others use all five in a single school. Two different mathematics programs are also offered: elementary school mathematics and a mathematics workshop.

Levels 6-8

A special set of objectives and TLU's is available to help older students master basic reading skills. This curriculum component, termed *Turning Point: High Interest/Low Vocabulary*, includes fifty TLU's and is for students with a history of reading deficiencies. It is integrated into PLAN*s computer system.

High School

The PLAN* secondary curriculum, for the ninth through the twelfth grades, provides a basic framework together with a broad spectrum of alternative strategies for individualizing instruction in language arts, mathematics, science, and social studies. The TLU's use of materials is flexible, which means they can be utilized with a broad range of instructional support materials available in most high schools, as opposed to being keyed into specific texts and instructional materials. The TLU's are course oriented and cover the following:

Language arts	Science	Mathematics	Social studies
English I	General/Earth science	General math	Geography/Civics
English II	Biology	Algebra I & II	World history
English III	Chemistry	Geometry	Contemporary issues
English IV	Physics	Trigonometry	Political/Economic
		Analytic geometry	systems
		Calculus	American history

Preschool or Kindergarten

Primary TLU's are designed to meet the special needs of children in their first three years of school. Instead of written directions, picture symbols are employed to show children what to use and what to do for each learning activity, thus making it possible for beginning readers to follow the directions on the TLU and work without constantly needing to be told what to do. These programs were developed to help teachers meet the needs of children aged three to five.

Individualized Program of Studies

PLAN* is individualized by developing POS for each student; the POS contains the objectives selected to meet his individual needs. The progress of the student is reported in terms of PLAN* objectives mastered, PLAN* objectives active (the TLU's on which he is working), and PLAN* objectives scheduled for future mastery.

The POS is developed from information concerning the student's past educational history, results of PLAN* Placement/Achievement Tests, and the teacher's knowledge of individual students. A new student is usually given an Interim POS based upon his classification at a particular achievement level in a subject. The Interim POS is modified by PLAN* Placement/Achievement test results that identify specific objectives a student has or has not mastered. The mastered objectives are filed in the computer as part of the student's completed POS; the nonmastered objectives are considered for inclusion in a student's POS. Once developed, the POS may be modified by the teacher should the student's achievement require it. The teacher, student, and parent jointly make decisions about a student's POS.

The Computer System

PLAN* provides a computer support system that does most of the record keeping and gives teachers more time to spend with children. In PLAN* the computer resembles an electronic bookkeeper; in no way does it replace teachers in providing instruction or making educational decisions. There are no computer consoles or other types of computer equipment in the classroom. Children learn from teachers, aides, and other students. The computer does the paperwork.

Here is how the computer support system works. Special computer cards are marked by teachers and students during school hours. At the end of the day these cards are fed into a reader that sends the information to a central computer in Iowa City, Iowa. After the computer has received all messages for the day, it processes the information, updates students' records, and prepares a report for each teacher. This report, the printout, is typed out on an automatic typewriter during the night and is ready for use by teachers and students the next morning.

Since the information is up to date each morning, the daily printout helps teachers in planning their activities. (For an example of computer printouts, see Figure 5-1.) Results of tests taken the day before are shown, along with a summary of each child's progress by subject area. The computer also helps teachers with long-range record keeping. As children complete objectives, a cumulative record is stored for each student by subject area. Six times a year, this cumulative record is printed out for use in reporting to parents.

By using the printout, a teacher can see at a glance which children need individual help or organized group discussions. Students use the printout to find partners to work with or a helper when they encounter problems.

The computer prepares a monthly administrative report detailing the progress made by students in each teacher's class and in the school as a whole. It puts an administrator in touch with exactly what is going on in every classroom in the building. A 177-page technical handbook, *The PLAN* Computer Manual*, provides answers to questions that come up in the daily operation of PLAN*.

```
DAILY REPORT          MATHEMATICS        MR. APPOLINARO        OCTOBER 13, 1973

ADAMO MARY BETH   (1213)  COMP 5004*  TESTED 2438-1  STARTED 2429-1*  SCH 2443-1, 2448-1, 2425-1
BAKER ROBERT      (7726)  COMP 2443-1  STARTED 2442-1, 2438-1*  SCH 2434-1, 2426-1, 2429-1
BYNOE DEBBIE      (1612)  COMP 2429-1  STARTED 2426-1*  SCH 2443-1, 2434-1, 2448-1
                          DELETED 2401-1, 2402, 2406-1
CHITES CHARLES    (1848)  COMP 2323-1*  TESTED 2317  SCH 2334-1, 2301-1
DAVIS WALTER      (2011)  TESTED 2411-1, 2425-1  STARTED 2434-1
GENSINGER JOHN    (5662)  COMP 2438-1  SCH 2414-1, 2440-1, 2442-1                          A
```

```
DAILY REPORT          MATHEMATICS        MR. APPOLINARO        OCTOBER 14, 1973

  2438-1  C O M P  GENSINGER JOHN, SERIPERRI VITO*   T E S T E D  ADAMO MARY BETH
          S T A R T E D  BAKER ROBERT, JACKSON WANDA, RALSTON IRENE, WALKER NED
          S C H  TAYLOR HELEN
  2440-1  C O M P  POWERS JANE, URIA AILEEN   T E S T E D  SERIPERRI VITO
          S T A R T E D  ORTIZ ELIZABETH   S C H  GENSINGER JOHN
  2443-1  C O M P  BAKER ROBERT   S T A R T E D  JACKSON WANDA   S C H  ADAMO MARY BETH,
          BYNOE DEBBIE
  2448-1  C O M P  POWERS JANE*   T E S T E D  WALKER NED*   S C H  ADAMO MARY BETH,
          BYNOE DEBBIE, TAYLOR HELEN                                                      B
```

A On any day of the week a teacher can choose to receive a printout organized by student (excellent for checking individual progress).

B Or by objective (exactly what a teacher needs to group students for discussion, review, or tutoring).

Figure 5-1
Examples of computer printouts

Dissemination and Use of the System

Following completion of the initial developmental work by the American Institutes for Research and the fourteen cooperating schools in July 1970, Westinghouse Learning Corporation assumed responsibility for marketing and continuing development of PLAN*.

The current edition of PLAN* for the instructional range of the first to the eighth grades has a base price of forty-two dollars per student, which includes all PLAN* documents in orientation and placement, language arts, mathematics, science, social studies, and the associated technical manuals for teachers and aministrators. Also included in the price are the following services: administrator training (ten-day workshop); teacher training (five-day workshop); daily computer processing (a printout in each subject area for each teacher); six periodic progress reports for each student in each subject area; computer processing of up to 200 locally developed objectives.

This price can be modified downward by having the local school district assume such responsibilities as printing TLU's from masters and using its own computer.

The cost of the commercially available instructional support materials is the responsibility of the local school district. In a new school with no support materials the cost is estimated to be about fifty dollars per student, which includes everything from books and workbooks to a wide range of audiovisual equipment and materials.

Most operating schools will already own the support materials. Though some items will have to be bought, costs will undoubtedly be much less than fifty dollars per child. It all depends on the present inventory. But, in any case, after the first year the cost of replacement and updating of materials will drop to between five and ten dollars per student.

During the school year 1973-1974 about 65,000 students were involved in PLAN*. About 40,000 were in the first to eighth grades, about 20,000 at the secondary level, and 5,000 in a special mathematics program for the fourth to the sixth grades. These students attended over 104 schools in nineteen states.

Evaluation Results from Users of PLAN*

The management component of PLAN* has a built-in system of accountability and evaluation. The progress and status of any individual student, group, classroom of students, or all students in a school can be summarized from information stored in the computer. Analysis and comparisons can be made with respect to time intervals, teachers, instructional program and the like. One user of PLAN* states: "We have a high degree of accountability now that we just could not have if we didn't have the management system PLAN* has."[8]

Superintendents and educators ask a number of important questions: "How does the academic achievement of students in PLAN* compare with that of students in traditional or other instructional programs?" "Is the difference PLAN* makes worth the financial cost of PLAN*?" "Is PLAN* better?"

Almost without exception, each school district involved in the program has set up some sort of project to evaluate the effectiveness of PLAN* to the satisfaction of members of the board of education, the superintendent, parents, and teachers. In some cases the project has been conducted by school staff members; in others it has been conducted by impartial outside organizations. While these projects vary, most of them are similar with respect to what was being evaluated, the principal areas being attitudes of parents and community toward PLAN*; attitudes of teachers and staff members toward PLAN*; attitudes of students toward PLAN*; the self-concept of PLAN* students; attitudes of PLAN* students toward school; achievement of PLAN* students; the degree of success of PLAN* in working with above average, average, and below average students. The remainder of this section will discuss these areas of evaluation.

Attitudes of Parents toward PLAN*

Almost without exception every PLAN* school conducts a survey on the attitudes of parents toward PLAN*, on their attitudes comparing PLAN* with the educational program prior to PLAN*, or on the attitudes of parents of children in PLAN* and control schools. The surveys show in most instances the individualized educational characteristics of PLAN* to be highly acceptable and usually preferred to traditional group instructional programs. Where surveys are made year after year there is a tendency for the acceptance of PLAN* to grow with each succeeding year. Though the results of most surveys are contained in reports for circulation within schools and for presentations to boards of education, some have been published. Eldredge, for example, reported the following with respect to the attitudes of parents: "Parents were at first quite negative toward the school program . . . . Later that year, parent questionnaires were submitted again. This time the reactions were quite different. The t value obtained to estimate the significance of differences in favor of the school was significant at the .005 level . . . . Additional comments written on the questionnaires were also very positive."[9]

A fourteen-item questionnaire was sent to 444 parents in Pleasant Valley, Iowa, during the initial year for PLAN* in the school. In response to the question "Have you noticed any changes in your child's attitude toward school this year?" 44 percent of the parents reported favorable changes, 23 percent reported unfavorable changes, and 33 percent reported no observable change. In answer to the question, "What do you like best about your child's school program this year?" the most frequent comment by parents was that their child was "not bored, could work at his own pace, and that PLAN* allowed for individual differences."[10]

At Ridgewood, New Jersey, the following results were obtained from a questionnaire to parents. When asked "Do you think PLAN* permits teachers to deal more effectively with individual students?" 75 percent said "Yes," 16 percent were "not sure," and 9 percent said "No." In response to the question "Do you think PLAN* helps to foster a positive student attitude toward learning?" 79 percent said "Yes," 13 percent were "not sure," and 8 percent said "No." While 79 percent were pleased that their child would continue PLAN* during the following year, 15 percent were "moderately pleased," and 6 percent were not pleased. PLAN* was considered to be a sound educational program by 76 percent, while 7 percent thought it was not. A total of 72 percent thought that PLAN* was a desirable improvement over the conventional form of schooling, while 10 percent disagreed with that view. When asked if PLAN* was sufficiently individualized to accommodate the needs of their child, 73 percent of the parents said "Yes," 18 percent gave moderate support, and 9 percent said "No."

Attitudes of Teachers toward PLAN*

An evaluative report for the John Muir Elementary School in Kirkland, Washington, gave results from two instruments used there.[12] *Indicators of Quality* measures quality in the school by observing certain critical aspects of behavior in the classroom.[13] As of June 1972, 30,000 observations in 224 school systems had been obtained in the *Indicators of Quality* project which was sponsored by the Institute of Administrative Research of Teachers College, Columbia University. At the John Muir School data were obtained indicating that the PLAN* portion of the school day had "an extremely healthy environment" and that individualization of instruction was a strength of PLAN*. The total score on the *Indicators of Quality* was reported to be the highest ever received in the Pacific Northwest on that instrument.

The second instrument used at this school was the *Purdue Teacher Opinionaire.*[14] Administered to all PLAN* teachers, the questionnaire yielded average subscores for that group, which were then expressed in terms of percentile norms for the test, the norms having been established on the basis of results in 250 schools. The percentile equivalents of average scores of forty PLAN* teachers at John Muir School are shown in Table 5-1.

Wilson sampled the attitudes of 234 first-year PLAN* teachers all over the country. Of them 79 percent felt that "students have a better learning experience in PLAN* than they had previously" and 73 percent agreed that "students in PLAN* develop a better self-concept."[15]

Interviews with PLAN* teachers supply evidence that the system is successful in providing desirable learning climates in the classroom and in promoting among students a sense of direct involvement in their educational development. Teachers in inner-city schools and in schools where minority students are in the majority comment that attendance increases, and truancy decreases; the pupils are happier, more independent, and work harder; disciplinary problems decrease; and there is a healthier classroom learning climate.

Attitudes of Students toward PLAN*

Studies conducted to assess modification of behavior and academic growth of students in PLAN* typically produce the following results: First, there is an increase in positive self-concept, particularly for minority students. Second, students develop more favorable attitudes toward school. Third, it is frequently difficult to detect much if any improvement in academic achievement by

Table 5-1
Percentile equivalents for mean scores of forty PLAN* teachers at John Muir School on the *Purdue Teacher Opinionaire*

Factors scored	Percentile
Teacher rapport with principal	99
Satisfaction with teaching	97
Rapport among teachers	99
Teacher salary	84
Teacher load	96
Curriculum issues	99
Teacher status	97
Community support of education	95
School facilities and services	99
Community pressures	99

students during the first year of operation. The lack of improvement is probably due to the fact that during the initial year students, teachers, and administrators are learning to operate a new instructional system. Many problems and interruptions occur, and the year as a whole is marked by some inefficiency. In the second and third years, however, efficiency increases, and academic gains become evident for PLAN* students in comparison with those in traditional instructional programs. The longer a student is in PLAN* the greater is the gain. A period of three years seems a good time interval from which to draw comparisons. Fourth, students who are average and below in ability appear to benefit most academically from PLAN*. For those who are above average, academic gains appear to be smaller. This may be due to the fact that "bright" students usually learn well regardless of what instructional system is used.

A number of studies support the above generalizations. An early survey conducted by AIR in one of the PLAN* cooperating schools evaluated gains in achievement over an eighteen-month interval, using analysis of covariance techniques to adjust for differences in ability between the PLAN* and non-PLAN* control students. Out of thirty-three comparisons, the performance of PLAN* students at Hicksville, New York, was superior to the performance of non-PLAN* students in twenty-five instances. In nine of these cases the differences were statistically significant; in four the performance of non-PLAN* students was superior to that of the PLAN* students; and in the remaining instances no differences were observed.[16]

Another study by AIR reported the effect of PLAN* and non-PLAN* instructional programs on increases in verbal scores over a two-year interval, concluding that "given a pattern of DAT-V and Cooperative Reading scores at Grade 9 the student will develop a higher verbal PSAT score at Grade 11 if he pursues the PLAN* program of studies than if he pursues the traditional program of studies. The advantage is greatest for the lower ability range and somewhat less at the higher ability range."[17]

The following achievement test results were reported for the Robert Frost Elementary School in Salt Lake City, Utah: "Preliminary testing after the first year indicated that PLAN* students were performing better than their peers in other schools in the district. In addition, they seemed to be better motivated, more independent, and happier than students observed in conventional classrooms."[18]

Goodview School in Winona, Minnesota, an elementary school with grades one through six, is in its third year with PLAN* and is being evaluated under a Title III grant. PLAN* sixth graders, on going to junior high school for the seventh grade, return to traditional group instruction. Since PLAN* sixth graders had not completed all of the TLU's classified at the sixth level, there was concern as to whether the gaps would be a handicap for them in the seventh grade. In a special phase of a study sixty-eight Goodview pupils, after a year in PLAN* in the sixth grade, did slightly better in the seventh grade (as determined by grade point averages) than did the sixty-one non-PLAN* pupils in a control group, even though the difference was not statistically significant. They appeared, therefore, to be successful in a traditional seventh-grade setting after their experiences in the individualized situation.[19]

A control group has been established at Winona. The mean intelligence quotient of this control group was 108, whereas the mean for the PLAN* students was 102, a difference found to be significant at the .01 level. When increases on the *Stanford Achievement Test* from spring 1972 to spring 1973 were compared for 224 PLAN* and 274 non-PLAN* students in the first through the fifth grades it was found that PLAN* students, on the average, showed 1.71 months greater growth during the school year than students in the control group.[20]

The most extensive evaluation of PLAN* is being conducted by the Foundation for Individualized Education and Research (FIER), an independent nonprofit research organization.[21] FIER has been under contract to six school districts that are now in their third year of PLAN*, and it is also conducting evaluations for four more school districts that have adopted PLAN* more recently. The evaluation program of FIER utilizes the *Self-Esteem Inventory*,[22] *General Anxiety Scale for Children*,[23] the *Test Anxiety Scale for Children*,[24] and the standardized achievement test used by the local school district. Comparisons are made, in most instances, between PLAN* and non-PLAN* students. The evaluation studies are in the nature of reports to school boards and the school community.

FIER has been evaluating PLAN* in the East Aurora, Illinois, schools where some 4,000 students are in PLAN*. A recent news item reported the progress of PLAN* students, stating that black and Spanish-speaking students, as well as their white classmates in individualized programs, were found to be learning better. While pupils of all ethnic backgrounds appeared to be improving, the black and

Latin children were closing the gap between their performance and that of the majority children. At the end of the first year a dramatic improvement in pupil self-esteem was noted, and improvement in academic performance was recorded at the end of the second year. The individualized program seemed to be helpful to all pupils.[25]

The most recent independent analysis of PLAN* was conducted by the Educational Products Information Exchange Institute (EPIE).[26] In its *Report Number 58* it stated that a high level of satisfaction existed among teachers and students using PLAN*.

Notes

1. Westinghouse Learning Corporation, PLAN*, 770 Lucerne Drive, Sunnyvale, California 94086.

2. John C. Flanagan, J. T. Dailey, F. B. Davis, I. Goldberg, C. A. Neyman, Jr., D. B. Orr, and M. L. Shaycroft, *The American High School Student*, Cooperative Research Project, No. 635, United States Office of Education (Pittsburgh: University of Pittsburgh, 1964).

3. John C. Flanagan and Steven M. Jung, *Progress in Education: A Sample Survey (1960-1970)* (Palo Alto, Calif.: American Institutes for Research, 1971), 28.

4. These school districts include Bethel Park School District, Bethel Park, Pennsylvania; Hicksville Public School District, Hicksville, Long Island, New York; Pittsburgh Public Schools, Pittsburgh, Pennsylvania; Quincy Public Schools, Quincy, Massachusetts; Wood County Schools, Parkersburg, West Virginia; Archdiocese of San Francisco, San Francisco, California; Fremont Unified School District, Fremont, California; San Carlos Elementary School District, San Carlos, California; San Jose City Unified School District, San Jose, California; Sequoia Union High School District, Redwood City, California; Union Elementary School District, San Jose, California; Penn-Trafford School District, Harrison City, Pennsylvania; Santa Clara Unified School District, Santa Clara, California; and Hughson Union High School District, Hughson, California.

5. Harvey J. Brudner, "Computer-Managed Instruction," *Science* 162 (November 1968): 970-76.

6. Available from American Institutes for Research, P.O. Box 1113, Palo Alto, California 94302.

7. *Behavioral Objectives: Science, Social Studies, Mathematics, Language Arts*, 4 vols., ed. John C. Flanagan, William M. Shanner, and Robert F. Mager (Palo Alto, Calif.: Westinghouse Learning Press, 1971).

8. Statement of Don Walker, principal of John Muir School, Kirkland, Washington.

9. J. Lloyd Eldredge, "An Evaluation of Project PLAN*," *Educational Technology* 13 (September 1973): 56-57.

10. Ed. D. Fauble, "PLAN* Evaluation," unpublished report of Pleasant View Elementary School, June 19, 1972, Pleasant Valley, Iowa.

11. *Ridgewood Schools at Work* 19 (November 1973): 3.

12. S. Michael Martin, *Plan* Evaluation at John Muir Elementary School* (Kirkland, Wash.: Lake Washington School District No. 414, 1973).

13. *Indicators of Quality: A Brochure* (New York: Institute of Administrative Research, Teachers College, Columbia University, 1968).

14. Ralph R. Bentley and Averno M. Rempel, *The Purdue Opinionaire* (West Lafayette, Ind.: University Bookstore, 1967).

15. E. Ida Wilson, "Survey of Attitudes of PLAN* Teachers," unpublished report, Bradley University, Peoria, Ill., 1972.

16. William M. Shanner, *Comparison of Performance between Intermediate Grade PLAN* and Non-PLAN* Students on Standardized Achievement Tests* (Palo Alto, Calif.: American Institutes of Research, 1971).

17. William M. Shanner, *PLAN*/NON-PLAN* Instruction as a Predictor of Preliminary Scholastic Aptitude Test Scores of the College Boards* (Palo Alto, Calif.: American Institutes of Research, 1971).

18. Eldredge, *op. cit.*

19. John Lewis, *Evaluation Report on the Second Year of the Winona Title III Project PLAN** (Winona, Minn.: Winona State College, 1973).

20. *Progress Report on the Evaluation of the Goodview Title III Project* (Winona, Minn.: Winona State College, 1972).

21. The Foundation is located at 248½ E. Lincoln Highway, DeKalb, Illinois 60115. Its director is Dr. Marvin Powell of Northern Illinois University.

22. Stanley Coopersmith, *The Antecedents of Self-Esteem* (San Francisco: W. H. Freeman, 1967), 265-66.

23. Seymour B. Sarason *et al.*, *Anxiety in Elementary School Children* (New York: John Wiley, 1960), 86-88, 306-10.

24. *Ibid.*, 92-94, 306-10.

25. *The Beacon-News* (Aurora, Ill.), December 23, 1973.

26. *EPIE Educational Products Report* 58 (New York: Educational Products Information Exchange Institute, 1974).

6. An Instructional Design Theorist Examines Individualized Instructional Systems

Leslie J. Briggs

An instructional design theorist is concerned with the identification of the process and technique of instruction and an understanding of the effects of the learning environment on individuals and groups. Although many traditional principles of learning derived from learning theories have demonstrated value, such as reinforcement, continuity, and repetition, instructional design theorists draw heavily on the works of Gagné and others who combine learning theory with concepts directly related to instructional design, such as conditions of learning, categories of instructional objectives, learning task analysis, and the interrelationship among these concepts.[1] This chapter examines the three individualized educational systems described in the preceding chapters from the above orientation.

Common Features of the Three Systems

The three individualized instructional systems have common features that suggest the meaning of "individualized instruction" to the developers of these systems. Among those characteristics are the following.

The emphasis is upon flexibility in teaching. Thus an effort is made to educate all children rather than to teach only those who fit a particular pattern of aptitudes, interests, and personal characteristics.

Each system uses a common core of objectives. While the three systems vary somewhat on this point, collectively they appear to assume that there are some core skills, such as in communication, which are needed by all, not only in order to qualify for further education but also to lead to a successful and happy life. In addition to these core objectives (expected of all or most children) self-selected or optional "excursion" objectives are also provided. Not all children are expected to complete or attempt the same entire set of objectives. Some latitude is allowed in choice of objectives and in expectations for number of objectives completed. The differences are clearly illustrated by Glaser and Rosner in Figures 4-1 to 4-4.

The systems are humane. While systems-based instruction is often thought to be "highly structured" and is often contrasted with "humanistic" approaches, both kinds of approaches can, and indeed do, treat children as individuals, and they both avoid interpretation of different goals or different rates of progress as "failure."

The systems do not limit the objectives. A common misconception is that preplanned, highly structured systems must, by nature, focus on trivial objectives. It is clear that the goals and objectives discussed in all three systems have varied as much as do objectives for other types of systems.

Attention is paid to the starting point. Each child is interviewed, tested, and counseled to determine his entry skills so that instruction may begin at a reasonable starting point. He does not, therefore, suffer the boredom of repeated exposure to objectives already mastered or the disappointment of failure because of starting at too advanced a level.

The three systems carefully and continuously monitor progress during the learning of a single objective and as the child moves from one objective to the next; thus, more up-to-date planning and diagnostic data are available than in most conventional systems. In two of the three systems the monitoring is facilitated by computer-managed instruction (CMI). PLAN* integrated CMI in its initial development, and IPI has recently done so.

Even though the systems are individualized, the child is not taught in isolation. Teachers take great care to vary activities appropriately among individual study, small-group activities, and large-group activities.

Each system employs predesigned materials. Whether called TLU's, "modules," or "units," the instructional materials and evaluative exercises are designed to allow different pupils to be working on different objectives and to enable students to be more self-directive. The nature of such units varies: some are designed to require little help from the teacher; some use self-instructional procedures such as programmed instruction; some concentrate on giving clear "directions to the learner." Though the providing of clear directions may suggest a structured approach, in another sense such directions may be seen as enabling the child to work more independently than in conventional "teacher-led" instruction. Self-pacing and branching features make independent work possible. To varying degrees the "instructional events" are designed into the materials themselves, or they occur as a result of materials or activities independent of the unit.

Formative evaluation is extensively used. The learner receives continuous feedback, which guides his progress and informs him of his accomplishments. The data from such feedback are used to improve the system itself. In addition, summative evaluations are planned. To this point, all have had a degree of summative evaluation, but some are in stages of development that make final evaluation premature.

Additional Features to Consider

It is possible for one concerned with instructional design to comment on other aspects of the instructional process that are either missing or are not prominent in the descriptions of the three individualized instructional programs.

In Chapter 1 Walberg contrasts the continental tradition with the Anglo-American tradition; the three systems of interest here are not clearly identified with either. They are less authoritarian than the conventional Anglo-American tradition, and they are designed for all children, not just the most "able." In overall characteristics, however, they adhere more to the Anglo-American than to the continental tradition.

The source of the goals is not entirely clear. While the three systems vary somewhat in this respect, it is difficult to determine whether the instruction is based on conventional goals or upon some new form of analysis of needs. All three systems emphasize adapting to the needs of students, but it is unclear whether these needs are identified by attempts to predict the future or by more conventional means. Though the closing sections of Chapter 3 represent the clearest rationale based on how skills in different domains are developed, one finds no reference to the work of the policy research centers as a possible basis for redefinition of goals and thus misses the "orientation toward the future" as discussed by Shane,[2] and by others in various issues of *The Futurist*. There is an emphasis upon preparing the child to be a competent and happy adult, but only in some future society, the nature of which is only cursorily discussed. Also, it is not clear whether the needs of the future society are compatible with perceived needs of today's children. One cannot criticize the three systems for not showing how the future can be forecast and used in definition of goals, but the absence of discussion of this possibility leaves one at a loss as to how goals were identified. The systems are not, of course, preoccupied with method to the neglect of content, but the rationale for the method is usually clearer than the rationale for the goals.

While the three chapters varied in explicitness about various categories of planned outcomes, none reported consistent use of a taxonomy to check upon the scope of coverage of objectives, test construction, and the planning of instruction. Though the reader may infer different domains of goals or planned outcomes from the three chapters, none showed clearly that different strategies of teaching resulted from use of a taxonomy. Most educators are familiar with the idea of using a taxonomy to classify objectives and to plan for procedures of evaluation, but few are as explicit as Gagné concerning the way a taxonomy can help build the conditions of learning into the events of instruction.[3] How this may be done for the total scope of educational objectives represented by a fivefold taxonomy is the major theme of a recent volume by Gagné and Briggs.[4] Nevertheless, the descriptions of two of the three systems show clear evidence that the different school subjects were in some systematic way seen as drawing, to varying degrees, upon diverse categories of learning. Such a procedure may have been involved in all three developmental efforts, but this was not made equally explicit in all three instances.

New materials were not always developed, particularly in the case of PLAN*, where the strategy was to employ existing materials in producing the learning units. The economic reason for this decision is, of course, obvious, but one could argue that it tends to limit the objectives of the program. Existing materials can indeed often be used for more than one objective by planning different ways to use the same materials, but if no materials exist for a desired objective, either the new objective must be abandoned or a special development effort must be undertaken, as was apparently done by PLAN* in some instances. Yet if one wishes to branch out into entirely new areas, the restriction upon new development could be a problem. It would, for example, be difficult to make a major curriculum thrust toward studying the present problems of our society, such as those listed by Shane, without the development of new materials.[5] One assumes, therefore, that such new objectives are perhaps more fully explored in the other two systems, which appear to have been oriented more to the development of new materials as a needed part of the projects. As some of the chapters suggest, however, much of the instruction in elementary schools is likely to focus upon the basic skills common to most curricula. The idea of new areas of study may become more important at the secondary and postsecondary levels.

Goal-free evaluation is not heavily emphasized. All three systems take behavioral objectives seriously. It is, indeed, a major merit of this type of program that one can set a design objective based on the attainment of explicitly stated performance objectives by the children. Thus one can plan for the majority of the students to attain a defined level of mastery on certain sets of objectives. This strategy embodies the important possibility that the system can meet its design objectives, and the designers can know when this has taken place. Attention to the intended outcomes of instruction could lead critics to suspect that unplanned outcomes are not detected and evaluated, but the creators of these systems do not have such a narrow outlook. Though little is said in the three accounts of the programs to convince the skeptic that these unexpected outcomes are of interest, dedication to the planned outcomes does not indicate that the developers of the systems do not plan to search for the unexpected outcomes or the side effects of instruction. These dedicated systems designers want their programs to impart a love for learning and an interest in the subjects studied; they also hope to produce competent learners.

One must conclude from the above that goal-free evaluation plays only a small part in planned summative evaluations. But it must be recognized that the three chapters focus upon development and formative evaluation. If the authors were asked to submit a summative evaluation plan, one may be sure that breadth of scope would be reflected in those plans. And, perhaps, this discussion of goal-free evaluation is premature since it is related primarily to stages of work not yet reached in the development and use of the three systems.

Suggestions for Future Developers of Individualized Systems

In light of the above comments, it would seem helpful to suggest some techniques that would aid in future efforts to develop systems for individualized instruction.

Forecasting Future Needs

This has been touched upon in at least two places earlier in this chapter. The real question is: How should an analysis of needs be made in order to give even greater relevance to educational programs of the future?

Some persons attempt to forecast our future by the Delphi method of analyzing consensus among experts concerning various aspects of the predicted future. Others employ different methods for attempting to depict the nature of life, work, and leisure in the future. The possibility of "future shock" is included in such discussions. These forecasts suggest possible curricular changes for future systems.

A number of educators, realizing the high risks involved in forecasts of the future, fall back upon the goal of teaching children to be adaptable problem solvers. They hope that in this way they can prepare students to solve problems that are not yet even perceived by the present generation of adults. Thus "lifelong learning" and "learning how to learn" become educational goals.

Three articles may be cited to illustrate forecasting of the future. Jones has undertaken to show how cable TV may change our lives in the fairly near future.[6] The educational implications of computer technology coupled with TV technology are portrayed by Baran, who envisions as a major resource of learning study stations located in homes, offices, libraries, and various other places.[7] These two articles discuss particularly the mode of learning in the future rather than the content to be learned. Ofeish has suggested that new systems of schooling are emerging.[8] He sees the downfall of the tradition-bound teacher and the survival of more flexible, creative teachers as the managers of future learning environments. If this forecast is accurate, perhaps the training received by teachers in the three individualized instructional programs will assist in the transition from present to future systems of education.

New Research and Development Procedures

Some of the theory used in current educational systems is based on experimental study of single variables in learning. The research paradigm for such studies is the "experimental group-control group" paradigm, in which the presence of a relationship between an independent and a dependent variable is established. Simon has pointed out that this paradigm ignores the strength of such relationships, and he states that psychophysics and operant conditioning are two types of research that do seek to determine the actual form of a functional relationship and the numerical values of its parameters.[9] He goes on to show how more information could be obtained from experiments in the area of learning. Since he is interested primarily in short-term memory, he sees no quick method for attaining such precision in the study of long-term memory and more complex cognitive functions.

In contrast, the theories of Bruner, Ausubel, and Gagné, while dealing perhaps at a somewhat more molar level, do seek, and, to many, give promise of, more rapid progress in research-based developments than is the case for the research recommended by Simon. Still other theorists, of course, see no immediate possibility of applying learning theory to curriculum development. They would then rely upon either intuition or empirical methods to develop new teaching strategies. Both Bruner and Gagné see the road to improved teaching, not through learning theory per se, but through techniques such as task analysis, learning hierarchies, and "spiral sequencing" of instruction.

In one effective instructional program little theory was employed; there was, instead, a common-sense rationale for selection of media, and there were repeated applications of empirical methods.[10] This program was designed to train employees of the Bell Telephone System in first aid; the heavily empirical methods did result in decreased training time and increased learning. Markle tested untrained personnel to discover what knowledge relevant to the objectives was already possessed by most adults in the target population. Thus fewer objectives were needed in the training program. Then by repeated use of a criterion-referenced test, methods and materials were developed to produce the most relevant learning in the shortest time. Markle first experimented with test questions and answers, carefully sequenced (again empirically determined), as a first crude learning program. When the subjects could not produce a criterion response, "instruction" was added. Thus, unnecessary material was kept out of the program, while the usual formative evaluation (test data) based on error scores was used to add or to modify content. While this program had a limited and clearly defined set of objectives and was not complicated by long-term goals as in education, its procedures still represent one of the best-known examples of the power of empirical trial and revision.

New Formative Evaluation Techniques

Markle's report gives a brief account of the use of response latency data as a formative evaluation technique. By using special equipment to present test questions and to record "reading time" as distinct from "answering time," Markle obtained precise data on average times and times for individuals. These techniques, developed initially by Brooks, employ response latency for the purposes of improving test items, arranging instructional sequencing, and improving first-draft instructional materials.[11] The conventional use of item analysis of errors on a criterion test helps show where more or better instruction is needed, but it does not detect irrelevant or unnecessarily redundant instruction. These procedures, as employed by Markle and Brooks, hold great promise, especially for the more "fine grained" improvements in educational programs.

One of areas where research is needed concerns the discovery and appraisal of new methods of formative evaluation. The techniques cited above refer primarily to the effectiveness and efficiency of instruction. Other techniques are required to improve acceptability and utility of individualized systems. One present need is for a compendium of techniques, such as those employed by Markle and Brooks, so that the greatest benefit can be derived from the methods of testing and revision. While one hopes for the emergence of better instructional theory, in the meantime the use of formative evaluation is one of the major strengths of the three systems described in this book.

Selection of Media

Choice of media remains, to date, mostly a matter of practicability and intuition in most educational systems. While such factors as costs, resources, the intended learning environment, and the attitude of teachers and pupils are all logical considerations, a few efforts have been made to systematize the basis for selection of media. Most such efforts attempt to match the choice of media with the characteristics of the learners, the type of objective, and the assumed learning environment.

Perhaps the best-known rationale for the choice of media is the "cone of experience" developed by Dale.[12] He lists twelve types of media in a somewhat age-related order, with reference to the target population. Young children would learn by "direct purposeful experience," such as by observing and manipulating real objects rather than symbols of them. As one goes up the scale, he encounters pictorial representation of objects and at the top symbolic learning, as in reading. This extremely useful scheme permits the designer to select a type of medium that is low enough on the scale to ensure adequate learning and high enough to ensure efficient learning. The "size of chunk" of instruction for which such choices are made is not prescribed.

A somewhat more analytical model for selection of media has been developed.[13] Samples of how this model works in practice are presented from examples of instructional design developed by graduate students. In this model (for the domain of intellectual skill) one first places each objective in a learning hierarchy. For each subordinate competency (enabling objective), one next classifies it by using the taxonomy developed by Gagné.[14] Then, for each competency, one lists the instructional events and the conditions of learning to be designed. A medium of instruction is selected for each such teaching step. Thus the "size of chunk" for the choice of media is not at the level of an entire objective, but rather for each teaching step for a subordinate competency. One first selects the type of stimuli desired, such as printed words or still pictures, and then any convenient medium by which such stimuli can be presented is a candidate for choice. It is the identification of the type of stimuli that is important; after that decision is made, any one of several "candidate media" can be chosen on basis of practical considerations. The series of media choices is then reviewed for the purpose of planning to change the media often enough to avoid boredom but not so frequently as to make the classroom procedure cumbersome or disruptive.

The selection of media is often based on what is believed to be best for the majority of a group of learners. But when resources permit provision for parallel media for the same objective, one can then attempt to select a medium for each individual learner. Guidelines from research are of some help in making these selections, but such guidelines must be supplemented by a study of the learner's past patterns of success when he worked with various media.[15] This was one reason for use of the computer in PLAN*.

Another analytical model is that by Tosti and Ball,[16] whose "presentation design variables" are somewhat analogous to Briggs's stimuli. They too feel that the specific (physical) medium chosen is not important as long as it fits the presentation design, and they discuss dimensions of presentation, such as intensity and duration of stimuli. While both these models emphasize stimuli, they also acknowledge the importance of student response and feedback; it would thus be a mistake to classify either as "stimulus oriented" if to do so implies neglect of response and feedback.

It appears, then, that future systems could be more systematic in their plans for the selection of media.

Sequencing of Instruction

Design models usually devote considerable attention to the provision of a sequencing of learning experiences designed to ensure successful learning. The specific rationale for such sequencing differs according to the theory upon which one is building. Several reviews have been made of these rationales. Briggs, for example, focuses upon sequencing for intellectual skills as represented in a learning hierarchy.[17] Gagné and Briggs have recently treated sequencing in all domains of learning, for the basis for sequencing varies among the domains. Examples of such sequencing for intellectual skills are given elsewhere.[18]

Instructional Strategies

Overall instructional strategies vary, of course, with the theory on which they are based. Chapter 1 of this book presents a comprehensive review of contrasting strategies.

In the model developed by Gagné and Briggs design of strategy is closely related to a learning taxonomy. Thus the instructional events are designed to incorporate the special conditions of learning shown to be applicable to each domain or subdomain of learning outcomes.

The Curriculum Base

In a draft of a working document for a seminar, I have developed a "dimensional analysis of alternate models for the design of instruction." This document is intended to aid students in classifying, comparing, and contrasting alternate design models. The major headings in this dimensional analysis are: "The Assumed Learning Environment"; "The Form of the Delivery System"; "The Design Model Employed"; "The Development Methodology"; "The Diffusion and Installation Plan"; "The Choices Made by Learner and by Designer (or Teacher)"; and "The Curriculum Basis."

Several of the above major headings either coincide with or cut across the way previous chapters in this book are organized. One could, for example, redescribe the three systems by using these headings. The dimensional analysis scheme is, as a whole, less general than the two traditions (continental and Anglo-American) contrasted in Chapter 1, and perhaps more inclusive than the four instructional design components in Table 2-1. Those four components (objectives, organization, modes of transaction, and evaluation) might be viewed as related to the "design model" category in the above dimensional analysis scheme.

Curricula have, by tradition, tended to be designed by specialists in the subject area. Some curricula are oriented toward learning the current content or knowledge developed by the discipline; some are based on the intellectual processes used in the discipline; some employ behavioral objectives; many, of course, attempt to develop problem-solving skills.

The suggestion here is that designers might reexamine proposals made over the years that organize curricula by the types of problems to be solved by society. This clearly implies a multidisciplinary basis for instructional design. If the actual solution of such problems requires multidisciplinary research, perhaps older students at least need a multidisciplinary curriculum.

Conclusion

This chapter is not intended as an evaluation of the three individualized educational systems. Its goal was, rather, to summarize some of the techniques the systems employ and to suggest some that might be employed in the future. The closing sections allowed the writer to go from consideration of these three particular systems to some speculation and reporting about matters of concern to an instructional design theorist.

Notes

1. Leslie J. Briggs *et al.*, *Instructional Media: A Procedure for the Design of Multi-Media Instruction, A Critical Review of Research, and Suggestions for Future Research* (Pittsburgh, Pa.: American Institutes for Research, 1966); Robert M. Gagné and Leslie J. Briggs, *Principles of Instructional Design* (New York: Holt, Rinehart, and Winston, 1974); Leslie J. Briggs, *Handbook of Procedures for the Design of Instruction* (Pittsburgh, Pa.: American Institutes for Research, 1970); Robert M. Gagné, *The Conditions of Learning*, 2d ed. (New York: Holt, Rinehart, and Winston, 1970).

2. Harold G. Shane, "The Educational Significance of the Future," a report prepared for the U.S. Commissioner of Education, Contract No. OEC-0-0354 (October 1972). Available from the World Future Society, Box 30369, Bethesda Station, Washington, D.C. 20014.

3. Gagné, *op. cit.*

4. Gagné and Briggs, *op. cit.*

5. Shane, *op. cit.*

6. Martin V. Jones, "How Cable TV May Change Our Lives," *The Futurist* 7 (October 1973): 196-201.

7. Paul Baran, "Thirty Services That Two-Way Television Can Provide," *ibid.*, 202-10.

8. Gabriel Ofeish, "The Future of American Education," *ibid.* (December 1973): 275.

9. Herbert A. Simon, "How Big Is a Chunk?" *Science* 183 (February 8, 1974): 482-88.

10. David G. Markle, "The Development of the Bell System First Aid and Personal Safety Course: An Exercise in the Application of Empirical Methods to Instructional System Design," mimeographed (Palo Alto, Calif.: American Institutes for Research, 1967).

11. *Ibid.*

12. Edgar Dale, *Audiovisual Methods in Teaching*, 3d ed. (New York: Holt, Rinehart, and Winston, 1969).

13. Briggs *et al., op. cit.*; Briggs, *op. cit.*; Leslie J. Briggs, *Student's Guide to Handbook of Procedures for the Design of Instruction* (Pittsburgh, Pa.: American Institutes for Research, 1972).

14. Gagné, *op. cit.*

15. Leslie J. Briggs, "Learner Variables and Educational Media," *Review of Educational Research* 38 (April 1968): 160-76.

16. D. T. Tosti and J. R. Ball, "A Behavioral Approach to Instructional Design and Media Selection," *AV Communication Review* 17 (1969): 5-25.

17. Leslie J. Briggs, *Sequencing of Instruction in Relation to Hierarchies of Competence* (Pittsburgh, Pa.: American Institutes for Research, 1968).

18. Gagné and Briggs, *op. cit.*; Gagné, *op. cit.*; Briggs, *Student's Guide to Handbook of Procedures.*

7. Affective Education: Fact and Fancy

Louis J. Rubin

What we are concerned with here is the relationship between the individualization of learning and something that has come to be called "affective education." Because the two conceptions have a logical—almost natural—congruence, it is appropriate that, in a volume devoted to the general problem of idiosyncratic learning, the matter of affect be considered, for nothing is quite so individualized as the ways in which we feel about ourselves and our world.

The quest for a true adaptive environment in schooling has long been the ultimate goal underlying much of our knowledge-generating and theory-building endeavors. It is not unseemly, for this reason, to speculate about the potential for individualizing emotional growth, and for attempting the curricular integration of cognition and affect. Elsewhere in these pages other authors have discussed the flexibility of instructional programs, the possibilities for adapting environments to specialized needs, psychological theories relating to individualization, and alternative systems for personalizing children's learning. No less than these, perhaps, affect constitutes a critical factor in the equation.

Our interest in affect derives chiefly from three principal issues: Do the learner's affective states have a bearing upon his cognitive achievement? Do his cognitive and affective mechanisms operate in tandem? When his emotional well-being is impaired, can school experiences serve as correctives? The last of these three issues involves two disparate factors: emotional liabilities incurred during life in school, and those resulting from traumas encountered in the world outside.

Affective and Humanistic Issues

It would be well, before considering these issues, to clarify—to the extent that the irregularities permit—the variform aims and aspirations of the "affective movement" itself. If the divergent objectives are not first set forth, we cannot attend to the larger task—judging whether a particular affective goal is attainable within the context of schooling—at least as we know it. Such clarification is difficult because, in recent times, many of the associated ideas have become meaningless shibboleths, camouflaging a lofty set of notions that are more mystique than anything else.

One reads, for example, of "humanistic education," "psychological education," "sensitivity training," "confluent education," "self-awareness training," and a variety of programmatic trappings aimed at value clarification, motivation, self-realization, joy, and (in those instances where even joy is insufficient) ecstasy.[1] It is not so much that these ambitions are unworthy (although their realization often is questionable), but rather that without reasonably precise definitions it is impossible to determine what is what.

To clear away the undergrowth, then, and at the risk of some oversimplification, it suffices to say that in the following arguments affect is meant to imply emotional tone or feeling. While scholarly thought on the matter is less than unanimous, the general presumption is that three reciprocal forces together constitute an affective state: bodily sensations involving the heart, stomach, skin, and so on (visceral afferent stimulation); the particular circumstance in which the individual finds himself, such as a burning building, a tense classroom, or a chair by the fireplace; and the specific thoughts the situation evokes in the person.[2] Such affective states as joy, anger, fear, and despondency normally result from the interplay among these three factors. It follows, accordingly, that, at least in a technical sense, affective education has to do with mood and emotion, with the antecedent conditions giving rise to these feelings, and with the consequent behavior the feelings generate. The clearest aspect of the movement lies in the work of the humanistic psychologists wherein personal experiences and inner concerns serve as the locus for improving affective adaptation.

Humanism, to touch upon the other quasi-generic name associated with the movement, suggests, in contrast, a curriculum dedicated to human welfare. But here, too, confusion is rampant. Some workers argue that an exposure to humanistic disciplines will increase the learner's commitment to humanism, whereas others suggest that humanistic experiences per se will make the learner more humane. If the literature as a whole is reduced to its pragmatic essence, the conception that probably comes closest to the heart of the matter is that the self is viewed not only with respect to personal fulfillment but also with respect to serving the human good.

Humanistic education embodies, in its broadest meaning, an entirely new conception of curriculum. The child must learn to look inward as well as outward; the cultural heritage, rather than absorbed whole, is to be bent in accordance with the needs of the present; individual concerns and personal autonomy are dominant goals in the learning program; and values are acquired, not as a social legacy, but through an examination of societal ills and a consideration of what constitutes the good life.

Thus, if we take the goals to be, in general terms, those of a healthy self-concept, a sense of well-being, the ability to cope with emotional susceptibilities, and a sound portfolio of values, the critical question thus becomes: are these feasible educational ends, or are they, instead, more akin to an impossible dream? We are obliged to remember, in pondering the answer, that we are living in a dark time when man is increasingly to be confronted with painfully difficult choices. These choices involve not the comparatively easy options of the past regarding "right against wrong," but the infinitely more treacherous questions of "right against right"—questions, in short, having to do with priorities among competing passions. Hence, the problem is not merely whether the ends can be achieved; it is also whether the costs of achievement are, in one way or another, prohibitive. A spate of related issues thus arises: Can the schools effectively counterbalance deleterious experiences accumulated earlier in a child's life history? If they can, moreover, do such efforts fall within the proper spectrum of the school's purpose? Are affective and cognitive objectives antithetical? Do affective objectives call for an unstructured environment and the improvisation of pedagogical methods? And, finally, to link the problem with other ideological conflicts, does affective education mitigate against compulsory schooling, against social indoctrination, against the use of competition, or against the inculcation of values?

The surest path to a sane conclusion regarding these issues seems to lie in an examination of the nature of affect. Unless the phenomenon itself is probed, little can be done to determine its utility. What then can be said—despite our imperfect knowledge—regarding affect and its relationship to curriculum?

The Nature of Affect

The literature is a bit inconsistent, and theorists vary somewhat in the meanings they attach to emotion and feeling, but for our purposes it seems legitimate to take the terms as interchangeable. Both refer essentially to the same behavioral dynamics.

Emotion seems to function as a control-gauge to the organism's state of well-being. Put another way, our feelings—whether of sadness or euphoria—trigger physiological reactions that organize our energies and order our behavioral inclinations. Depending upon whether these inclinations are simple or difficult, possible or impossible, our emotions, in cycle, respond accordingly. Since emotion is involved both in prompting behavior and in reactions to the aftereffects of the behavior, we probably cannot, properly speaking, divide behavior-inducing emotion from reactive emotion.

The same emotional state may, moreover, arouse different behavior in different people. Frustrated by the events in the classroom, for example, one child grows apathetic while another responds with heightened drive. Further, as every teacher knows, children—like their adult models—develop negatively oriented and positively oriented emotions over both authentic and counterfeit (illusionary) circumstances. Yet, because the counterfeit always seems real, they respond as if it were real. For example, the child who misreads the signs and believes her teacher does not like her responds emotionally as though she were being rejected. It is largely for this reason that affect is so closely interwoven with the individual's perception of his experiences. It is not stress, in short, but rather the way the person responds to the stress that largely sets the antecedent conditions of emotion.

Untold amounts of psychological damage probably accrue in the nation's classrooms as a consequence of such misperceptions. Because a student seems indolent or lazy, rebellious or hostile, the teacher makes demands that are intended to produce behavioral change. But if in fact the student is neither lazy nor rebellious, but rather is acting to forestall failure, to enhance a sense of status, or to manufacture even artificial feelings of independence, then, in a classic circularity, the teacher's demands are resisted, emotions of even greater intensity are unleased on both sides, and the combat is enlarged.

Emotions serve useful purposes. Varying in both nature and intensity, they stimulate feelings of pleasantness and unpleasantness, content and discontent, hatred and love. The quest for sustained ecstasy is, therefore, not only impossible but impractical as well; when one is caught in an uncomfortable situation, there is more to be said for acting to change circumstances than for self-deception leading to a fraudulent impression of joy. Unpleasant emotion stimulates us to adapt our behavior and to take actions that may reduce our discomfort. Until our affective states become sufficiently pathological to disable us, they have a functional utility. All of us discover relatively early in life that the surest way of terminating disagreeable emotion, if we can, is to isolate the cause and either remove ourselves or counterattack—to fight, in short, or to flee. It is precisely this mechanism that tempts so many adolescents, in the face of unsuccessful school experience, to drop out. Rather than adapt, or even rebel, they turn elsewhere for satisfaction.

One implication of all this, at least for the curriculum designer, is that if affective education does have a place, it ought not be aimed at inducing a false sense of emotional contentment either by distorting reality or by mindlessly seeking to replace uncomfortable emotion with comfortable. It should, instead, equip the individual to fend for himself and to acquire cognitive coping skills with which to manage the emotional entanglements that inevitably occur throughout life.

The nature of these cognitive coping skills, as we shall shortly see, varies according to individual and setting. They cannot be taught as universals because what works for one person may not for another.

The strongest clue to a pedagogical tactic for accommodating such individuality may lie in asking why—emotionally—one child's poison is another's cup of tea. Why, in brief, is one person traumatized by an incident while another emerges unscathed?

Attitude and Affect

A part of the answer, for the psychologist, rests in the extraordinary impact of what is termed attitude. Attitudes are intimately bound up with affective states precisely because our needs, our expectations, and our desires, as well as the emotions set loose when these are facilitated or impeded, are all heavily influenced by what we value and believe and by the attitudes created by these values and beliefs. Our attitudes, in sum, virtually make us what we are. Consider, for example, Allport's celebrated words on the matter:

> Without guiding attitudes, the individual is confused and baffled. Some kind of preparation is essential before he can make a satisfactory observation, pass suitable judgment, or make any but the most primitive reflex type of response. Attitudes determine for each individual what he will see and hear, what he will think and what he will do. To borrow a phrase from William James, they "engender meaning upon the world; they draw lines about and segregate an otherwise chaotic environment; they are our methods for finding our way about in an ambiguous universe."[3]

Attitudes, as Lewin observed, establish the determinants in the largest part of our encounters in life: they fashion our opinions regarding the trivial and the sublime; they create the scales on which we weigh and assess the behavior of those around us; and they profoundly influence our goals and aspirations. For both the child in the classroom and the elder in the rest home, then, attitudes define the phenomenon that principally occupies us here: individuality. It is the infinite variation in the shades and intensities of our attitudes that, more than anything else, makes us unique.

Although scholarly thought on the function of attitude is less than unanimous, there is relatively widespread agreement with Allport's basic premise that attitudes are learned predispositions to respond to situations in consistent patterns. This "consistency of conduct," to use his own phrase, suggests that children are not likely to alter their behavior until a prerequisite shift in attitude has occurred. Hence we can tentatively hypothesize that, since attitudes predispose one to behave in certain ways, the dominant thrust of affective education should focus upon the child's attitudes and, concomitantly, on the beliefs that give them form.

Suppose, for example, a teacher believes (cognition) that permitting children to chew gum impairs the discipline of the classroom. In view of this belief, she may form the attitude (behavioral predisposition) that permitting children to chew gum in class is wrong. Now, presuming that no other factor mitigates against the acting out of this attitude, she likely will prohibit her students from gum chewing. Suppose, however, that the principal does not believe that gum chewing is bad, that the teacher thinks that the principal must be pleased if she is to receive tenure, and that the teacher believes that securing tenure is all important. Under these circumstances she will probably permit rather than prohibit gum chewing. We are forced to conclude, consequently, that while attitudes generally are indicative of probable behavior, they are not always so. Thus, as Fishbein has demonstrated in recent attitudinal research,[4] any given attitude, isolated from the individual's apperceptive mass, may or may not be predictive of either intended or actual behavior. What this means, therefore, is that in seeking to nurture improvements in the child's affective life, we cannot deal with simple cause and effect, but must, instead, allow for a variety of contingencies and assume multiple causation. It also means that we must deal first with the way the child appraises and reacts to a situation—with the antecedent conditions that cause him to interpret it as threatening or benign—and second with the behavior provoked by the response to stimuli.

It is plain, then, that cognition and affect create their own continuous loop. Cognition (belief and perception) is a powerful influence in shaping attitudes, and attitudes, because they define what we see as good or bad in a given situation, play a large part in directing the nature of our emotional responses. In any given emotional encounter, the individual responds to stimuli that are cognitively perceived, cognitively assessed, and cognitively interpreted. As Schachter states,

an emotional state may be considered a function of a state of physiological arousal and of a cognition appropriate to this state of arousal. The cognitions arising from the immediate situation and interpreted by past experience provide the framework within which one understands and labels his feelings. It is cognition which determines whether the state of physiological arousal will be labeled "anger," "joy," or whatever.[5]

Put another way, when we are beset with an emotion-inducing circumstance, we first perceive the relevant stimulus conditions; next, we assess their probable consequence; and, finally, we interpret the meaning of these assessed implications so as to determine a course of action. What we choose as rational action, however, is shaped by our attitudes regarding what is desirable and undesirable.

As Schachter tells us, however, these interpretations are also colored by our recollection of previous experiences. Memory, in other words, is cognitively based, incorporating a collection of notions that involve values, expectations, and attitudinal predispositions.

The selection of appropriate responses to a situation is also congitively inspired in that the individual must, in one way or another, "reason through" a course of action. Hence, what we may term cognitive processing, or cognizing, includes, as Lazarus has suggested, an interpretational, or "meaning giving" function, and a decisional or "response generating" function, both of which are filtered through a recollective membrane stemming from past events. Lazarus postulates, in fact, two specific processes of appraisal:

One, which is called primary appraisal, deals with the issue of threat or non-threat. The other, referred to as secondary appraisal, has to do with the possible alternative ways of coping with the threat and the conditions relative to coping. However, once threat appraisal takes place, information about possible lines of coping (secondary appraisal) is given urgency, or search processes relevant to coping are activated. These appraisal processes should not be regarded as necessarily consecutive in time but rather as involving different sources of information on which coping decisions can be predicted.[6]

These processes of appraisal are made even more difficult by two habitual sources of error. First, the recollective membrane, through which perceived stimuli are assessed, is a relatively unreliable filter. Since our capacity for dealing with information is limited, what is sometimes called "cognitive overload" (an informational mass exceeding the individual's capability of managing it) may result in behavioral decisions that ignore vital cues that are present. Second, efficient cognitive processing is further impaired whenever the recollective membrane fails to consider significant aspects of past experience. All of this means that irrational behavior may stem from the improper decoding of a situation because essential information has either been disregarded or forgotten. Bruner concludes, moreover, that since interpretation is essentially "an act of categorization,"[7] a third source of error may exist. If errors of assessment occur in the "categorizing act," behavior generated through the interpretational and decisional processes may similarly be fraught with error.

To complicate matters further, the cognitive processing of perceptual stimuli also involves what Kemmis[8] has labeled the integrative function. As stimuli are appraised, the organism seeks not only meaning that fits the specific situation, but one that is compatible with the overall system of beliefs as well. This integrative function is, in a sense, akin to Piaget's conception of equilibration; Festinger's theory of dissonance-reduction; Rogers' construction regarding the organization of self; and White's arguments concerning cognitive motivation. Disequilibrium occurs when a coherent pattern of meaning cannot be derived from the assessment of perceived stimuli or when there are contradictions between the immediate assessment and similar assessments in the past. The individual seeks to reduce disequilibrium by resolving, through some workable form of integration, his cognitive conflicts. Conflict is avoided in some instances through withdrawal—a kind of walking away from the situation. The perceived discrepancy may, in other instances, induce stronger integrative efforts and, at times, corresponding cognitive revisions.

While individuals can sustain and survive cognitive discrepancies (conflicting expectations, incompatible beliefs, and symbolic incongruities), a deep-seated inclination to seek integration nonetheless seems to exist. It is worth noting, parenthetically, that mild discrepancy may have its own virtue. Langer,[9] for example, sees disequilibrium as essential to change, and Ginsburg and Opper[10] view mild arousal as an incentive to a coping approach. But, since invalid meanings and premature resolutions can often satisfy the individual's need to reduce discrepancy, additional possibilities of cognitive error are brought into play.

Finally, before we return to the main theme, it would be useful to note the important curricular distinction between education and therapy. Although fertile in its potential bounty, affective education borders upon a Promethean ambition. There is an abiding danger that we may go beyond the pale. It is perhaps legitimate to aim at a curriculum that enables students to acquire rational beliefs, good perceptual accuracy, and effective methods of dealing with emotional crises. To go beyond these goals—to aim at specific therapy, for a specific child, in a specific crisis—however, would be to trespass on foreign soil, to ignore our fundamental responsibility, and to exceed our talents. The preventive aspects of affective education are, in short, much more defensible and manageable than the treatment aspects.

Thus, to return to the central argument, we have found that cognition and affect interact in multiple ways; attitudes are bent and shaped through cognitive inputs; and—because of their capacity to establish behavioral predispositions—attitudes influence the perceptions (accurate or inaccurate) that in turn kindle emotion. Two additional elements now must be considered before the case for affective education can be consolidated into a conclusion: the ties between attitude and self-concept, and those between self-concept and need.

Attitude and Self-Concept

The Germans have a word, *Weltanschauung*, used to summarize the individual's attitudes toward himself, his life, and his purpose. All of us, to recall an ancient psychological principle, tend to conceive of ourselves according to the particular interpretations we place upon the meaning of our accumulated experience. In evaluating this experience, we obey a kind of inner logic which is conditioned by our attitudinal repertory. Our self-concept, then, is the gestalt of the personal attitudes we hold regarding ourselves. It is these attitudes that serve to order and direct our behavior. A relatively competent person may have a defective self-concept, while a relatively incompetent one may have a comparatively healthy self-concept. Where estimates of self-worth are concerned, therefore, it is not what we are, but what we think we are that is important.

Each of us is impelled by a profound desire to function effectively—to make use of our talents, to do what we do well, and so to earn esteem among our associates. For if we are not considered worthy by those whose opinions we value, if we do not have a secure sense of belonging to and being accepted by the social groups in which we find ourselves, if we cannot both give and receive affection, it is almost impossible either to think well of ourselves or to be content with our lives. It is hardly surprising, therefore, that, because of the potency of these needs, a considerable amount of affective disturbance is bred when they are not met. Frustration, anxiety,

depression, and similar emotional states are the inevitable consequence of negative affects set loose by a deficient self-concept, by
the inability to cope with problems from which there is no escape, or
by some other manifestation of ungratified psychological need. Thus,
in a tragic and perpetual pendulum, bad experiences spawn painful
emotion, and, in the counterswing, disabling emotions generate more
debilitating experience.

Inevitably, then, the child's perceptions, beliefs, and attitudes regarding self—his *Weltanschauung*—are an indispensable component in
affective education. Indeed, a basic tenet of humanistic psychology is
that "all behavior is a function of the perceptions existing for any
individual at the moment of his behaving, especially those perceptions he has of himself and of the world in which he is operating."[11]
It is in this postulation that we encounter the great ideological and
curricular paradox: should the curriculum emphasize substantive
knowledge, coping skills with which to control unpleasant emotion,
the individual's feelings regarding sense of self, purpose, and life-style
in the environmental milieu, or—if they can be fused—some combination of all three? The issue is, of course, more philosophical than
methodological. The hard question is: what are the relative benefits
of knowing one's self as opposed to knowing, say, Euclidean geometry? And, the philosophical issue aside, is it not also possible that a
psychologically inappropriate process of learning Euclidean geometry
and the resulting failure to learn may themselves have a damaging
effect upon the learner's self-concept.

It also seems fair to argue, in connection with self-concept, that
curricular efforts to individualize instruction must acknowledge that
the child in the classroom—no less than his adult counterpart—is
heavily driven by self-interest. We are all, in a sense, self-seeking,
profoundly interested in achieving whatever we think is to our advantage, and energized by equally profound desires to avoid whatever
is to our disadvantage. It is sometimes easy to forget, for example,
that children are functioning organisms susceptible to the same range
of emotion as their elders; there is little real difference emotionally
between the infant coveting a toy and the man coveting a sports car
or the girl threatened by an examination and the woman threatened
by a divorce.

A teacher's efforts to guide affective growth, and to improve self-
concept, are greatly complicated by the fact that the relationship

between attitude and behavior is not one to one; that is, both negatively oriented and positively oriented feelings are complex adaptive
reactions stemming from an assortment of influences. We cannot
assume, therefore, that two children manifesting similar behavior are
motivated by the same attitudes, beliefs, or values. One girl studies
diligently because she sees personal benefit in the knowledge gained,
whereas another is motivated by the wish to acquire a good grade.
Each, nonetheless, acts in accordance with perceived self-interests.
Hence, the attitudes governing one's emotional contentment are
compulsory material in the individualization of affective education.

When we extend the analysis further and probe the deeper implications of the student's need to protect or improve his psychological
lot in life—and, concomitantly, his self-concept—still another principle of significance to affective education emerges. If the school
endeavors to help children strengthen their emotional muscle, and to
better the ways in which they act out psychological needs, we must
recognize that any new behavior arising out of an attitudinal change
not only must fit their personal circumstances, but must also produce consequences that the children themselves regard as satisfactory. To achieve a healthy affective state, desires must either be
gratified, delayed, or eliminated. The boy, for example, who, feeling
ignored and rejected, creates classroom disturbances so as to gain
attention is not likely to adopt new forms of behavior unless they
too generate the desired attention, or unless an attitudinal shift
diminishes his need for attention. Similarly, the girl who must endure
a hostile and suspicious father, debilitated by his own emotional
shortcomings, cannot successfully adopt any behavioral pattern that
does not permit her to deal, realistically, with the father's moods. It
is because we *are* self-seeking, in brief, that we enact adaptive and
maladaptive behavior that seems to fit both our situations and our
self-conceptions. Our actions are need oriented precisely because we
are inclined to do what we feel we must do.

The logical outgrowth of need-oriented behavior, obviously, is that
the individual's reactions to events in his life are not fixed, but rather
vary from circumstance to circumstance. The emotions, in a word,
are fickle. A woman, tyrannical as a mother, is docile as a wife; a boy
is a nuisance in one class and a model of cooperation in another; a
principal is authoritarian with teachers and deferential with the
custodial staff. Depending upon our appraisal of a situation, our

needs, and our concept of self, we draw particular attitudes to the fore, and consequent emotions may erupt. All of which is to say that it would be folly—in the name of affective education—to indoctrinate children, as has sometimes been tried, with a catechism of prescribed emotional responses to typical situations in life.

The Individuality of Need

Since there are few places where individuality is more apparent than in the arena of personal need, the common ground between affect and the individualization of instruction is undeniable. We differ not only in our emotional architecture, but in the nature of our accumulated experiences and in our perception of the situations in which we find ourselves. There is, thus, great variation in human need—variation that accounts for the vast contrariety of our affective responses. We are so affectively disparate, in fact, that emotion probably can only be observed, or inferred, from responsive behavior; the emotions yield up their secrets only grudgingly.

Having briefly explored the larger dimensions of the topic, we can now review, both by connecting loose ends and by setting the stage for some conclusions regarding the role of schooling in affective education, the dominant factors involved. The reader may find fault with a perhaps overly tedious recital of old ideas—viewing them as thrice-told tales—but they have seemed to me an essential backdrop for the case to be made.

Our emotions serve useful functions. Feelings, falling along a continuum ranging from very bad to very good, exert great influence on our behavior. We adjust our actions, in effect, so as to increase the likelihood of positive affective states and decrease the likelihood of negative ones. These intuitive adjustments, consequently, depend upon our conceptions of what is important, upon the way we interpret past experience, and upon the cognitively ordered and attitudinally influenced decisions we make regarding motor adaptation.

Emotional adaptations, whether good or bad, stem from the interplay of our needs, the requirements of the situations in which we find ourselves, and our experience-conditioned attitudes regarding appropriate behavior in the situation. "Emotion," says Pribram, "expresses the relationship between perception and action."[12]

Because of the dynamic interplay among situation, need, and

attitude, emotionally inspired behavior is completely idiosyncratic. We cannot, therefore, generalize about either the specific consequences of belief and attitude or the specific antecedents of behavior. People exhibit similar behavior despite differences in attitudinal outlook; they develop parallel attitudes despite contrasting experiences; and they act out different behavior even where there are similarities in attitude and experience. Our affective adaptations are, seemingly, as exclusive as our fingerprints.

The relationship between cognition and affect derives, in part, from our personal conceptions of our needs. Beyond the fixed primary needs (essential to the maintenance of life), the secondary needs (essential to a wholesome self-concept and a feeling of well-being) are influenced by our beliefs. Beliefs (values) and attitudes (predispositions to behave in certain ways) are therefore manifestations of what we consider significant in life. Individuality in affect is, therefore, ordained by uniqueness of the organism's nature and circumstance.

We may infer, consequently, that emotionally inspired behavior is learned behavior and that learned behavior can be unlearned and replaced with different behavior under certain circumstances: the new behavior is congruent with the individual's beliefs and values; it is appropriate to the reality of his situations; and it is personally gratifying. Finally, cognition and affect create their own homeostatic feedback loop if only because cognition is the mediating force between stimuli and affective response.

The Case for Affective Education

Life in school provides its own cultural milieu. Teacher and child, as well as child and child, interact in a cross section of interpersonal relationships which engender the full range of human feelings. Three propositions therefore follow: school experiences may produce negatively oriented emotional liabilities; negatively oriented emotions may diminish learning achievement; and the use of compensating or preventive mechanisms may—at least theoretically—overcome these liabilities. Preventive measures can be initiated by efforts to make the psychological environment of the school more hospitable, and compensating mechanisms can be initiated by dealing, child by child, with the particular perceptions, interpretations, and attitudes bearing upon the affective difficulties that arise. When we turn, however, to emotional susceptibilities, born of encounters outside the school, the odds lengthen considerably.

For one thing, long-standing affective habits leading to maladaptive behavior are not easily amended; for another, the child's apperceptive mass, in most instances, is so rigid that school-designed interventions may come to little more than inconsequential tinkering; and, beyond these limitations, such interventions probably require a professional finesse exceeding the training of most teachers. The most imposing restriction is that it is impossible for the school to control the experiences that create and nurture emotional difficulties when the student is not in school.

All of this is not to say, however, that, putting therapeutic interventions aside, the curriculum cannot incorporate a variety of constructive exercises that improve affective adaptation. Using representational and symbolic materials, for example, students can sharpen their perceptual skills and enhance their cue-utilization abilities. Lessons that facilitate the analysis and clarification of values can be deployed almost everywhere in the instructional program through the examination of emotion generating situations—drawn from literature, history, and politics. The individual student's attitudinal mindset can thus be brought into the open and subjected to self-scrutiny. Alternative behavioral adaptations to emotion-laden situations can be compared, permitting the learner to contrast different coping strategies in both the appraisal and response phases. And, generally, many of the cognitive-processing skills themselves can be strengthened through systematic and carefully evaluated practice.

It is perhaps worth noting that most of the current affective educational projects tend to emphasize self-awareness, self-perception, and self-concept ideals, without adequate attention to the related cognitive processing. Such preoccupation with self is understandable since most of us find our personal concerns interesting, but the emphasis is not without pitfalls. Without true commitment on the part of the learner, the programs are reduced to little more than games; the ventures are made precarious by the absence of a systematic instructional methodology, thereby inhibiting the training of teachers; and it is conceivable that, at least in some instances, the programs may increase rather than decrease a child's sense of anxiety. Yet one occasionally finds, in the classrooms of gifted teachers, remarkably constructive gains being made. Like so much else in teaching, much depends upon the artistry of the practitioner. There is, however, a great need for carefully developed instructional materials and for corresponding teacher-training programs that deal explicitly with the cognizing aspects of coping and adaptation.

Whether affective goals should be substituted for the substantive objectives of the traditional curriculum is, of course, a matter of considerable dispute. The answer to the issue hangs, obviously, upon one's definition of the proper functions of schools. It is clear that time devoted to a consideration of "self" or to coping mechanisms reduces the time available for the teaching of a specific subject. Some subject matter can, of course, be pressed into dual service. The study of a great novel, for example, may allow the learner to grasp the relationship between human expectation and the consequences of ungratified need or to contrast personal values with those characterized by the author. Such a compromise does not, however, go far enough to satisfy those who believe that affective education is, in itself, a primary purpose of schooling. Those who see the school as a place for transmitting the wisdom of the past regard affective education at best as much ado about nothing and at worst as a waste of precious time.

With respect to the possible contradictions between affective and cognitive goals, therefore, the answer again depends upon philosophical preferences. Affect, as we have seen, does mandate considerable cognitive activity involving the skills of perception, analysis, synthesis, interpretation, and decision making. These, however, contribute only indirectly to the capacity for processing historical facts, understanding scientific phenomena, or using mathematical equations. As in the case of open education, fundamental ideological choices must be made.

Aesthetics, the arts, and the humanities provide, perhaps, an exception. Here, the content itself reflects feeling, symbolism, the expressive domains, and—obliquely—values. Much might be gained from extending their curricular treatment because they are now seriously understated, they are pertinent to the spiritual malaise that characterizes our times, and they lend themselves to feeling and emotional expression. But one must, at the same time, acknowledge that there is a patent difference between mood evoked by art or music and that invoked by psychological disequilibrium.

Somewhat firmer answers may be possible for the remaining questions. There seems to be little reason, for example, to assume that affective education necessitates an open environment—at least if an open environment is taken to mean an unstructured, child-centered curriculum utilizing random, freely improvised teaching methods. The cognitive processing of affective stimuli, emotional coping skills, and positive self-concept all can be dealt with either in a structured or an unstructured setting. It is essential, of course, that in either case the learning environment itself must not have a negative affect, but one cannot logically argue that a traditional curriculum must, of necessity, malign the spirit, bore the senses, or abuse the dignity.

The obligatory use of extemporaneous teaching methods in affective education is similarly questionable. Aside from the fact that good teachers habitually invent tactics to fit their needs—whatever the curriculum design—the extreme precariousness of working with the emotional life, alone, would seem to demand carefully tested techniques and thoroughly trained teachers, sensitive to the fine line separating legitimate and illegitimate interventions.

I have not touched, in this discussion, upon a field that is closely related to affective education—humanism. It suffices to say that the conventional program of instruction is, in this regard, undoubtedly guilty of serious sins of omission: there is little concern for the individual; preoccupation with thought drowns feeling; the matters of personal ethos and personal experience are largely ignored; and self-fulfillment is left mostly to chance. These, too, must have their due.

It is not hard to detect, even among the less alienated young, the darksome mood and despairing sentiments of our days. All is far from well with the society, but if man is perfectible, as many assume, the time is ripe for constructive pursuits. Properly conceived, affective education could serve as an ameliorating movement. Without descending fully into the revisionist bog, one can hardly deny that the present treatment of emotion in the curriculum constitutes a deficiency sorely in need of attention.

Notes

1. Mario Fantini, "Humanizing the Humanism Movement," *Phi Delta Kappan* 55 (February 1974): 400-402.

2. Irving L. Janis *et al.*, *Personality: Dynamics, Development and Assessment* (New York: Harcourt, Brace and World, 1969).

3. Gordon W. Allport, "Attitudes," in *Handbook of Social Psychology*, ed. Carl Murchison (Worcester, Mass.: Clark University Press, 1935).

4. Martin Fishbein, "The Relationship between Beliefs, Attitudes, and Behavior," in *Cognitive Consistency*, ed. Shel Feldman (New York: Academic Press, 1966).

5. Stanley Schachter, "The Interaction of Cognitive and Physiological Determinants of Emotional State," in *Anxiety and Behavior*, ed. Charles D. Spielberger (New York: Academic Press, 1966), 194-95.

6. R. S. Lazarus, "Emotions and Adaptation: Conceptual and Empirical Relations," in *Nebraska Symposium on Motivation, 1968*, ed. W. J. Arnold (Lincoln, Nebraska: University of Nebraska Press, 1968), 175-266.

7. Jerome S. Bruner, "On Perceptual Readiness," *Psychological Review* 64 (January 1957): 123-52.

8. Stephen Kemmis, "Another Look at Anxiety or Coming to Know Medusa's Face," unpublished paper, 1973.

9. Jonas Langer, "Disequilibrium as a Source of Development," in *Trends and Issues in Developmental Psychology*, ed. Paul Mussen, Jonas Langer, and Martin Covington (New York: Holt, Rinehart and Winston, 1969).

10. Herbert Ginsburg and Sylvia Opper, *Piaget's Theory of Intellectual Development* (Englewood Cliffs, N.J.: Prentice-Hall, 1969).

11. Arthur W. Combs, Donald L. Avila, and William Purkey, *Helping Relationships: Basic Concepts for the Helping Professions* (Boston: Allyn & Bacon, 1971).

12. Karl Pibram, "The New Neurology and the Biology of Emotion: A Structural Approach," *American Psychologist* 22 (October 1967): 834.

8. Problems and Prospects for Individualization

Michael Scriven

Introduction

Perhaps the best way to illustrate the problems with individualization and the prospects of solving them would be to review each of the contributions to this book. Having been asked not to do this by the editor—and there is a case for keeping books separate from their reviews—I turn instead to a more general review of the scene, based on some years of study of evaluations and samples of content of many individualization programs. This is more fun because I do not have to document every shocking revelation or allegation. Also, it takes much less time, especially since the only way to be sure one is not making unfair remarks about the previous chapters is by not reading them. Lastly, I think that a discussion of general issues is much more likely to be readable, especially but I hope not only for the authors of the earlier chapters.

The General Scene

There are good pedagogical reasons for moving toward individualization, there are good political reasons, and there are the usual reasons. The pedagogical reasons include respect for individual differences in learning styles (that is, abandonment of unjustifiable assumptions about "normal" rates of learning and development). The political reasons (those applying only because of a certain political situation) include the attempt to salvage an adequate education for the good or average student in the face of attacks on grouping based on ability because it produces grouping based on race. The usual reasons include its relative novelty, the positive connotations of the term, pressure from the originating organizations, funds for experimental implementation, and endorsement by large numbers of prestigious figures. It is important to note that what I call the usual reasons are about the same here as they are for competency-based training, behavioral objectives, criterion-referenced testing, resource centers, and responsive environments. The vast pendulum of educational fashions ticktocks its way through these semantic miasmas with a malign lack of concern for the modest real merits of each innovation. Its time has come; enthusiasm waxes. The time has gone; we swing to other things. There is nothing in education that fills me with the horror that pendulum inspires. It is the metronome of mediocrity, the crude clock that marks our lost chances of progress, and, I think, of survival. Once we have wound up this great engine, with all the forces of fashion and faddism, it is no easy task to slow it down, to get its cadence into step with the instruments that measure quality. The clock ticks on, and movements come and go to its beat.

Individualization is now on the upswing, perhaps approaching its peak. It has run into snags, and there is a certain disillusionment about, as the rabbits discover that this game, too, is imperfect. Their little noses begin to twitch, hoping to catch the scent of a new sport. Will the next few years see them hop away, or can we retain enough of them long enough to provide a critical mass for continued development of the useful forms of implementation?

Whatever the public relations answer, whatever the sociology of knowledge suggests, there is only one professionally or ethically acceptable answer, and that is to encourage the identification and demonstration of merit (or its lack) wherever it is to be found in individualization projects and practices and to encourage adopters and disseminators to respond to merit when making their decisions. That is why most of this essay is about evaluation. There are various experts who can assist with the training of adopters in the skills of evaluation and with the encouragement of adopters in employing those skills. But there is little ground on which to build that effort if we do not have some really solid evaluations of these projects in the first place.

If we are to get away from the worship of the pendulum, we must first develop a stable capacity to identify dependable virtues in educational processes and products. That will not be enough, but it is a necessary condition and one that is within our power as developers, funders, and evaluators to control. The second factor is the extent to which other people, adopters and consumers, will use demonstrated quality as a guidepost. If, however, we do not do that ourselves (or, what is worse, do not know how to do it), we are not going to be interested in their doing it, and they will not have a very good example to follow. I see at the moment no alternative future besides one of gradually increasing disillusionment with education and its products, replicating precisely the rise of consumerism and its skepticism about business. Nor do I see much reason to think this unjustified. Many people in education look as if they want to compete with Madison Avenue at its own level in selling products. The words they prefer are "disseminating" and "diffusing," but the right word is "selling." They generally convey an aura that combines elements of (a) avant-garde reality orientation, pragmatism, catching up with the rest of the world; (b) a mystique that suggests something above the common activities of the marketplace (this is where the jargon comes in handy); and (c) a kind of dedication to serving the schoolchildren of the world, a mission in which they are benevolently inclined to think that federal agencies should collaborate by subsidizing their advertising. These considerations are not necessarily, nor completely, incompatible. What is more worrisome is partly that the tensions between them have not been thought out and is mainly that they apply just as well to educational publishers and audiovisual hardware hustlers. I cannot see why the homely old criteria for federal subsidy of development do not exhaustively cover federal support of distribution: that is, the product would not be developed or distributed by private enterprise, and—the forgotten part—it must be so good that the use of a large slice of tax money on it is justified. The general problem with the big federally funded individualization projects, which have cost the taxpayer many fortunes to develop, is that they do not seem good enough to warrant the expenditures, and one begins to suspect, therefore, that the reason the private sector does not distribute the product is precisely because it is not that good.

Putting it once again, the only professionally tolerable justification for these individualization systems—for using them, developing them further, or pushing them—is their superiority over the homegrown or marketplace individualization offerings. And it is very hard to show that superiority if you never run a matched comparison group where the treatment *is* the best commercial package, or the best bet as the best commercial package (the bet being made by commercial or neutral sources, not by the system's producers). And of course the same arguments apply, mutatis mutandis, to commercial packages.

Now, most of these projects say that they have done well in field tests, but I am skeptical. One might argue that, in most cases, the educational significance of the actual gains, even using a no-treatment or old-treatment control group, has been very slight, a fact often buried beneath the incantations of statistical significance. I have already argued that the use of such a control is inadequate; there must also be a comparison with other possible adoptions, notably those already available. But let us look at the crucial factor for many prospective users of these systems—cost. The level of cost analysis being done on them is (I believe I am up to date on this) exceedingly primitive, especially with regard to indirect costs, and always noncredible, that is, always done or controlled by the staff of the project. I fail to see how the education profession can feel good about the stupendous and continuing development, costs of many of these systems when there is so little of the appropriate kind of evidence that they are worth even their current purchase price, let alone the initial investment.

Individualization is not, of course, the same thing as the big individualization projects. But, as this volume accurately reflects, they are a big slice of the power behind and the visible portion of individualization in K-12 education today. And—a crucial point—they have, and have always had, the resources for the kind of evaluation I have been discussing. Smaller efforts have at least the excuse of poverty, though it is a feeble excuse, since we are not talking about costs or difficulties that go beyond what the average college instructor can manage in his or her own or an experimental K-12 classroom.

Nothing said so far implies that individualization never does any good or never does good from a cost-effectiveness standpoint. There is much evidence that it sometimes works. But I believe that most of that evidence comes from installations of the Keller Plan or materials from BRL (Behavioral Research Laboratories). Very little of it has previously come from the plans represented by contributors to this book. The claims are much bigger than the successes.

What troubles me is the feeling that workers in this area, as in most such areas of innovations development, are too greatly inspired by the breakthrough paradigm and too little inspired by what might be called the breakdown paradigm. The truth on which the latter paradigm is based is that usually we learn much more about the real value of new apparatus when it breaks down than when it is running. My hero is the apocryphal individual who ripped the reel of paper out of a teaching machine that continuously malfunctioned, chopped it into page lengths, clipped them together, and ran this (was it the first?) programmed text against the teaching machines—successfully! When I see multimedia approaches being touted, what I think of as the ideal is someone lecturing while using a blackboard—*medieval* multimedia—not only because of the innumerable problems of breakdown of more modern multimedia but because I know of no case where the best such performer has been outperformed by the best multimedia show on anything but simply entertainment variables, and not on many of those (for self-selected audiences).

Simplicity is one hell of a powerful advantage for any educational process (and most others). When one is being seduced by the charms of even a tiny item like an overhead projector, a little voice should be muttering in one's head: "What happens when it breaks down?" That was the little voice no one was listening to when the foundations stuffed a few million dollars into Airborne TV (remember old Airborne?). It has its relevance to the individualization systems, especially to the record-keeping part of them, and most especially to the computerized record-keeping versions.

But perhaps the breakdown paradigm is too negative an alternative to offer to the inspiring thought of a breakthrough. There must be some image connected with progress—*cautious* progress—that could serve to inspire sensible work in education, which so rarely, if ever, produces anything that could reasonably be called a breakthrough. Perhaps we should christen the new concept the "seepthrough," which indicates the proper way to go—slowly. There *is* progress in education, not usually correctly located and more of it obtained as a result of breakdowns than breakthroughs, but it occurs—drip by drip. The book and the blackboard were breakthroughs, as was, possibly, the ball-point pen, at least for left-handed students and all parents and janitors who used to clean up inkblots. After the breakthroughs comes the seepage. Programmed texts can be a step up from regular texts, though most are not. And the day may come when computer-assisted instruction (CAI) seeps past programmed texts—somewhere. (Notice, though, that one should compare CAI with a good programmed text, not just a good text. The standard of comparison has seeped upward slightly.)

Computer-managed instruction (CMI), especially computer-assisted testing (test correction, construction, and record keeping), should make us look lasciviously at the well-managed grade book and card-filed item pool. If I got positively dizzy in lust for gadgetry, I would wonder whether edge-punched cards could not be smuggled in somehow as the new standard of comparison for CMI.

Individualization has, of course, always been with us. Indeed, that is what the one-room schoolhouse we have been racing away from was all about. The hoped-for breakthrough was envisaged as the result of *systematically managed* individualization *in many dimensions* with *specially developed materials*. What is not clear is whether, for the same amount of money, group activities of a fairly conventional (single-paced) kind could not have matched even the most optimistic gains claimed by the systems. The actual gains chiefly consist, I suspect, of gains for the *project*, resulting from investing a tremendous amount of money to finance some enthusiast's pet enterprise.

Apart from the rather nebulous gain of spreading the Chilling Effect, it would be better to compare systematically managed innovations with classrooms, schools, and school systems that adhere to the normal amount of individualization rather than to compare them with nonindividualized innovative treatment. In addition, as previously mentioned, one must make comparisons with other innovations along the individualization spectrum, especially those of lower cost.

PLAN* is unique in that it utilizes previously available materials as its core; it was not cheap to develop, but it avoided at least one kind of duplication of cost. For the other systems and those to be developed in the future the important question is whether there is any real justification for devising completely new content. The crucial questions are whether the content is good, whether it is better in one individualization project than another, and whether it is better in any of them than in the nonindividualized curricula. Though one often has the impression that content is assessed in a very impressionistic manner when new projects are being justified, my reading of the evidence (for example, in the evaluations of the Physical Science Study Committee and Project Physics materials) is that only huge, crude differences in content, format, and so forth show up in student behavior as educationally significant. I believe that content analysis can be a completely sufficient, though not ideal, basis for elimination or introduction of a curriculum (such as in the areas of "values education," which inconsistently teach that value judgments are not objective like scientific judgments and that we should all respect the rights of others to express their views in discussion). Thus I do not feel that it should be treated as secondary to articulation of modules. But it is equally bad to ignore interjudge reliability about content, which, I am afraid, was ignored in making many content decisions for the big projects. I see, in short, the individualization movement as beset by many of the same "problems of the pendulum" that characterize most of the movements in education. I see it swinging especially between the exaggeration of its value in order to keep up with each new fashion and the inevitable disheartening recognition that the promised marvels have not been flawlessly achieved. Excesses in either direction set education back.

The Case of PSI (Personalized System of Instruction): Some Particular Issues

In the earlier chapters in this book—to judge from the line or two on each sent me by the editor—little time is devoted to the Keller Plan; thus I shall use that as a specific example. (Any reader not familiar with this postsecondary cousin of IPI, IGE, and PLAN* should consult the excellent article by Donald A. Cook in *EPIE Educational Products Report*, 61 [April 1974].) Of all the systems, this one has, in my judgment, the most going for it, with its heavy emphasis on student-mediated instruction, usually high-quality content, better-motivated students, higher evaluation orientation, frequent use of programmed material, and large visible effects on affective and cognitive dimensions. I believe that something of a revolution in college teaching, and the attitudes toward it by faculty and students, is coming in on the wings of PSI. This is not to say, of course, that the revolution would not have found another vehicle; the time was ripe for it.

There are, however, still many things to worry about, including most of the general concerns mentioned in the last section. It may be useful at this point to make these concerns more specific.

Of the score or so concerns mentioned here, about half are not (as far as I know) publicly acknowledged as problems by those advocating PSI. We can begin with some that are, because of their importance and relevance to K-12 systems. Among them are the problems of space, time, and staffing. Space; the need is for controlled, monopolized, centralized, stocked, secure, flexible, and subdividable space, which is an expensive order. Time; students are often in time binds with the registrar on incomplete grades and find it difficult to apportion their time for studying and for other work; teaching assistants have heavy time commitments and typically need credits, which their teaching does not provide them; the faculty needs time to develop and revise the courses and to interact with their teaching assistants, which usually adds up to well over the normal course load, and so they also want course credit for the sessions with these assistants, but traditional institutions are unwilling to grant it. Staff; faculty often encounter severe hostility and reprisals from their peers, and teaching assistants are often not easy to get and to pay at the "classical" ratio of one for every ten students. These all represent costs of one kind or another (cash or credits) for one impacted population or another.

There are special problems with cheaters and procrastinators. In some areas of the humanities the social dimension of class attendance, limited though it often seems, is sometimes an important lost factor motivating attendance; there are particular problems with incorporating current issues (especially the occurrences of the previous day) and class discussions into PSI. As yet there is an extremely poor conceptual analysis of the significance of releasing test items in advance. The tendency to think that hardware technology, especially computers, is an appropriate early choice for supplementary help, instead of a last resort, is overly strong. Little serious effort is made

to get good cost-benefit or cost-effectiveness analyses for each installation and particularly for model ones. The research typically uses
outcome scores instead of gain scores, does not use random assignment, and does not involve varying the examining procedure, which
might reveal a large artifactual component in the good results. The
PSI movement is ignorant of the K-12 individualization systems (not
that they are much more informed about PSI), which is a real
absurdity since both have much to learn from each other. And,
finally, there are some ideological hang-ups, such as the popular
incantations about PSI being derived from Skinnerian learning
theory. In almost any sense in which that is true, "derived from"
simply means "suggested by," as are a great many other instructional
procedures that do not work.

I suspect that the relation between Skinnerian theory and PSI is
more nearly the reverse one, and possibly nearer still to the relation
between the knowledge of structural engineering of the master
masons who built Notre Dame or Salisbury Cathedral and the medieval version of statics, that is, the relation of "knowing how" to
"knowing (wrongly) why." It is not incidental that Keller's work
with intensive teaching of Morse code antedates his development of
PSI. The idea that PSI is "derived from" learning theory suggests that
learning theory is an accurate enough formulation to lead to PSI
procedures as a consequence, while not leading to alternative procedures. It suggests, conversely, that no other approach to the
scientific study of learning could account for the PSI results as well. I
think that both implications are false and that they greatly encourage
criticism of those who use PSI as endorsing or joining the Skinnerian
behaviorist camp, which restricts the spread of a good teaching
method for bad reasons. A more general problem is that something is
made to look scientific that is at most technological, and—what is
often the case in life and rarely in tests—the technology is what
works, not the "scientific theory." One might want to say, alterna-
tively, that theories in psychology at the moment are only mnemon-
ics. (That is what I would say, but it is not accepted by most of those
who talk of PSI as grounded in learning theory.) *Then*, of course,
there is no question of one excluding another nor of derivation in the
sense that it applies within the classical sciences. One way or another,
the ideological barriers that act to exclude those who feel nervous
about "laws governing human behavior," or even more nervous about

Skinnerian behaviorism, need to come down. Perhaps the simplest way to do this is to show that the usual humanistic ideology (customarily perceived by supporters as anti-Skinnerian) provides about as good a "derivation" of PSI as Skinner. Some elements of that argument are provided below.

Individualization as a Moral Imperative and an Economic Impossibility

Standard forms of education involve a fairly heavy cost to the student, usually justified as a means to avoid overburdening the taxpayer. Recent economic problems have led to increases in tuition and other fees in colleges throughout the country. In almost every case corresponding increases in scholarship funds have been grossly inadequate to compensate poor and middle-income families. The U.S. position concerning the equality of opportunity in higher education has thus continued to deteriorate in relation to that of, say, Britain, with the solitary exception of access for some minorities in some areas. It is a common fable in this country to suppose that this drift to elitism is recent, or only threatening now; it was, in fact, already severe twenty years ago. But the financial aspect is only part of the story; there are many other costs for the student hidden in the American system compared to the Oxbridge tutorial system, which can be considered one ideal in the college area. It must be remembered that attending lectures at Oxbridge is not required; that several lecturers speak on one subject from different viewpoints; that a tutor guides each individual at his or her own pace through the syllabus; that the examinations are externally set (that is, are not set by the tutors); that examination questions from all previous years are publicly available; that individual written work is required each week from each student and is discussed individually. It is fairly accurate to say that PSI approximates the Oxbridge model, and, while in some ways it improves upon that system, in others it is inferior. In any case, the similarities of the most ancient humanistic paradigm to the latest scientific one are quite striking.

From the moral point of view, to pick up another perspective, the student should (ideally) be treated as an individual, that is, he should not be shackled to the learning pace of other members of the class, should not be advanced without having grasped the prerequisites for the next lessons, should have a chance to ask questions without the risk of looking foolish in front of his peers, should be informed of exactly the kind of question and answer that he or she is expected to be able to handle, should get feedback on progress regularly, and should not have to attend lectures if learning is as effective and more convenient via other inputs. Only economic and other moral constraints can justify abandoning any of these points (in a weak sense, "rights"). What the individualization programs do is to show that significant improvement toward this ideal is possible within traditional settings, but not without some changes in the settings and the roles of those in them, as all "individualizers" know. But the real catch, apart from resistance to these changes, is that the cost of individualization is not generalizable. One can, for example, establish a PSI program here and there on a campus by filling in the interstices in the regular program (by utilizing an underused room or adding a teaching practicum for upper-class undergraduates), without unmanageable marginal costs. But to find a general solution, one must pick up great differences in cost, for which large sums of money are not likely to be available now, and one must solve serious unsolved problems in the system. One might say that PSI involves large negative economies of scale. (There are minor qualifications to this in some dimensions with some individualization programs, for example, with regard to sharing the cost of a computer.)

Thus to encourage strongly the use of PSI or any other system as providing students with their rights is very superficial since no one has a clear right to increase local taxes by, say, 25 percent to improve his or her education.

There is, however, a way to cut other costs so that PSI can be used widely within the existing budget: it involves aggregating small classes to make large PSI "classes"; dropping members of the faculty who teach small classes; and using unpaid teaching assistants in their place. Though the last part of this seems morally dubious, the paying of teaching assistants triples the salary cost for a class of one hundred students, in addition to which there are other high nonsalary costs. Not only are there no free lunches in education, there are few free crumbs. The cost situation is not nearly this serious for IPI *et al.*, but it is significant enough to make generalization within present budgets almost impossible.

For the external evaluator, therefore, and hence for the rational consumer and the principled disseminator, the crucial problem for individualization in the future will be to find ways to improve its cost-effectiveness, especially for wide-scale adoption. This is a task for which enthusiasm is not enough. Perhaps this essay will be useful in indicating both the size of the problem and the directions in which one must move to solve it.

NOV 2 1977
DISCHARGED

JUL DISCHARGED

DISCHARGED 1978

JUL 2 3 1980

DISCHARGED 1980
JUL 2 1980 ED

JUN 2 7 1979
DISCHARGED

DISCHARGED 1981

DISCHARGED
NOV 1981

RESERVE

DISCHARGED

RESERVE

DISCHARGED
DISRESERVE

DISCHARGED
DISCHARGED

DISCHARGED
RESERVE
FEB 2 1984
DISCHARGED

DISCHARGED
DEC 4 1984

RESERVE
DISCHARGED

8 1987
DISCHARGED